T0197344

MY JOURNEY OF LIFE WITH GOD

Poverty to Prosperity

Calvin L Bender

 www.trafford.com

North America & international
toll-free: 1 888 232 4444 (USA & Canada)
phone: 250 383 6864 ✦ fax: 812 355 4082

TABLE OF CONTENTS

INTRODUCTION

We all have our share of problems in life. Trials, tribulations, short comings, and issues, but the difference between success and failure in handling these inevitable parts of life is how we deal with it. Will we run from it, face it, or sweep it under the rug and pretend it doesn't exist or maybe it will go away on its own. If we chose to face it and deal with it head on samurai style, then we are already a winner. Even if we lose in the situation whatever it might be, we already defeated our worst enemy, our self.

But if we chose to run from an issue and continue to be in denial about how screwed up we really are, then we will be defeated. Everything we touch and everything we speak too will be defeated as well. We will destroy our self and every one we encounter. Like the old saying goes misery loves company and we love to make people feel the way we feel at times. And though when you first meet someone they seem nice and likeable or maybe even friendly at first, but after you get to know them for a while you eventually see the real person hiding behind the mask. By this time we have already been lied to, or they have lied on you, cheated on you, or treated you like dirt for no reason at all. These things or maybe even something worse has happened, but it all happens when we chose to ignore the hurt and pain people in our past have caused. That in turn may cause us to do the same thing to other people we may meet later on in life including our own family.

This is what happened in my life. And is one of the inspirations in writing about what I went through, how I dealt with it, and most important of all, how I got through it. I hope this book proves an inspiration for others in that no matter how far you have gone wrong, as long as you have breath in your life, you can make things right.

CHAPTER 1
The End

I was just a boy growing up in a small town in west Texas called Sweetwater. And at some point in time while living in this small Texas town I thought to myself while looking at everything around me "where did all of this come from?" and "how did we all get here?" I was always curious to the stars above and studied them on my own off to myself at night. One day I convinced my grandpa to buy me a telescope so I could go see all of the constellations, which was not a problem out in west Texas due to the wide open expanse of almost nothing. Anyway he did and I loved that white telescope that took me to the stars. It had me asking the question again "who made all of these stars?" I became really fascinated on planets and stars after seeing Halley's Comet at about three or four o'clock on a chilly morning in 1986. That Nike check sign looking light changed my view on the planet and solar system and my question "who made all we can see?" forever. So after we were hit by a tornado in the same year (by the way that tornado we were involved in was one of the scariest moments in my life). My mom moved us (my two brothers and myself) up north to live where my grandmother lived in a twice the size of Sweetwater town called Logansport in Indiana. This was like having a mid-life crisis, because I was in the middle of puberty, about fourteen years old. Moving from the south to the north was like moving to another planet as far as I was concerned. But yes, I said when momma asked each of us if we wanted to go to Indiana with her or stay in Texas with our dad. What was I thinking moving from all my friends in Texas to a place I knew nothing about? And then I had to make new friends. Well the reason I decided to go was because I could count all of my friends on one hand or so I thought. And two my dad in I did not see eye to eye most of the time. Anyway I always felt different being around other people and most times I was more comfortable being by myself. Yet I always wanted to be around the opposite sex for some reason. It was weird, but it was like I was more comfortable being around girls than guys. Anyway back to Indiana and the question that lingered in the back of my mind as long as I can remember. "Who created all of us and what we can see?"

One day while chilling at home I picked up a King James Bible I had in my room, why? I am still wondering why I had it in there myself, but still, I was curious. So I began reading the first book of Genesis and found that I could not get past the first chapter. I had not a clue what this book was talking about and I could not understand half of the words "thus", "thou" and the other. I had been to church before and realized that this was the book people would read from while in service. But it just did not make any sense to me. Little did I know at the time that I was closer to answering my question than I had ever been before? All the while I was becoming more reclusive in my own skin and around other people in my school. As I got older the lack of a positive role model began taking its toll on my attitude on life, affecting my relationships all around me from my freshman year of high school and on. When I was just six years old my mom and dad got a divorce and though I remember myself some of the reasons why, it really confused me. My dad was rarely around my brothers and myself and when he was it was like he wasn't if you know what I mean. If you don't know what I mean let's just say we could be in the same room and not have much to say to each other. So we never had a deep father son talk like I needed as a teenager about things I eventually would learn the wrong and hard way in the streets. Sex, money, and how to treat other people even if they treated you different, would have been a real good place to start back in those vital teenage years. This really molded my negative attitude on life. And anyone in the way of my life felt just how selfish a person can be without a positive role model. I can remember one time before we moved to Indiana I could hear my mom always complaining about how my dad was not paying enough child support and how we never had any money for this or that. I really felt bad for my mom. I mean at the time I had no idea whose fault it was that had us in the position we were in. So I decided one day that I was going to steal one of his checks from his check book and write a check so we could have some money. And so, that is what I did. Down to the last detail I had planned in my head from taking it to cashing it. It worked until I found out I missed the final detail; the fact the bank sends the check back to the original owner. Uh oh, I was in trouble not only with my dad, but with the law. Remember when I said my dad and I didn't talk much, well this was one of those times. And this was one of many lessons I had to learn the hard way. My dad got the cops involved. And I thought for sure I was going to jail at the age of thirteen by the way the detective was talking, but my dad wanted to prove a point. And he succeeded, because I was scared out my britches and he could have pressed charges. As a kid I was always thinking one step ahead, but negatively. And it was always this negative attitude that got me caught up in some of my own devious schemes.

Learning the Hard Way

I remember my sophomore year of high school when I went to live with my dad back in Texas. I found living up north to much for a Texas boy. The kids made fun of my ascent, I was not getting along with my mom, and I believe I was just having a bit of culture shock from being in Indiana. Going back home seemed to be the most logical answer at the time, so I thought. Anyway one day I had too much time on my hand and thought why take the bus to school when I can, well, drive. My dad's car that is, because "surely he would never find out while he was at work that I took it, or would he?" After a couple of days of planning, (that's all it took for my well thought out plans to take action) the mission was a go. No need for the details. The bottom line is I took my dad's Cadillac Eldorado to school without his permission. Oh and if that was not enough. Not only did I take it more than once, but I also tried to impress some girl on another block behind my dad's house with a ride to school. What do hormones really do to a young fellow with a mischievous mind? Long story short our town of Sweetwater is not all that big. So it did not take long for someone to spot me driving my dad's car down the road and two second's for him to figure out it had to be me. Another mistake of many I made that did not help my relationship out with my dad. Well, I suppose I will move on from this situation right into something else without learning my lesson. Just how stubborn can a teenage boy be? Never ask that question. I know I was plenty stubborn hind sight being 20/20. My dad had a collection of "movies" in a drawer in his room better known as "movies". And how in the blazes did I know that you may ask, duh. The same way I took the car, by plotting and scheming. I call it searching for answers, but careful what you look for you just might find it. I had access to well, um self-indulgence and where did this indulgence come from? That is a million dollar questions. Without a doubt is one of my biggest issues in life that took me away from my beginning question quicker than a raging forest fire. After the tornado in 1986, and before we moved to Indiana, my mom moved us to a neighborhood called Circle Drive. While there I was searching through things like I always found myself doing. I stumbled upon a box that just happened to have some, "magazines" in it. A thirteen year old discovering "magazines" and what else that thing could do between my legs, I might as well have found gold. I had just unlocked the dormant demon hidden within my inner self and it was a big one I must add. Before I go on with this I have to go back to the beginning, because finding adult magazines was not the beginning. The beginning was a seven, eight, or nine year old little boy on Hughes Street in Sweetwater that I no doubt had most of my memorable experiences. Let's go into the "hood" better known as the projects, because without shame is what all of our neighborhoods were that we lived in, projects. Ok so when I was like seven, eight, or nine more like seven or eight years old. I had girls on my mind. And like everything else I searched for I examined these creatures relentlessly. I had to have at least one at all times. So in the first grade and I do believe it is a good place to start. For one it is the beginning memory of my first "specimen" or girlfriend. Two why not start there? I can laugh about this now, but in reality this was a very serious thing, I will go on. This girl, and I will not name any names whatsoever (to protect the innocent), was the first girl I played house with. We didn't just play house we carried our pretend down to the last degree. I have no idea how I talked this girl into going to third base, but it happened. And even worse why did I even want to in the first place I was supposed to be more interested in building blocks. I was supposed to be into making believe. But dang that was very serious under that first grade desk and it sparked a major, major fire. I am just glad I did not have the sense to take it to home plate. Turns out it was a fire I had since birth and I was in trouble from the start. Back on the block I had this other "friend" and we would examine each other in the bushes. I would also examine our babysitter who would let me look and touch her stuff under covers, but this is not about re-living my child hood drama. This is about my journey and getting to the meat and potatoes of it. At the end of the day I had a problem with sex, which leads me back to the day I found the porn magazines and discovered myself. I found out what I was capable of as a teenager. But with the proper guidance I could have tamed it way better than finding out the answers the hard way, and on my own. What followed next was a trail of disaster which molded my life completely in a different direction than my initial question "who made us and why are we here?"

In the months and years to follow I would go through high school with an abortion on my conscience and plenty of people ticked severally off at me. This abortion is very sensitive to me and to protect the innocent will not at all be discussed. I would go into the Marine Corps after high school get married have a son and then come out eventually with a bankruptcy and a divorce. I would go through half a dozen relationships after or during this time. Coming out with two more kids which by the way molded how I got where I am now, my journey of life with God.

Military Experience

After high school in 1991 I immediately embarked on a journey I will never forget as long as I have breath. The first stop on the adventure without a doubt would have to be the United States Marine Corps. This by far was more of a challenge than graduating high school. Which was a miracle in itself for me due to the fact that, well, let's just say I had my mind on other things. The Marine Corps however changed my focus and perspective on life real quick. Before I went in, my recruiter shared with me a movie called Full Metal Jacket that had me second guessing my enlistment decision. The beginning of the movie though entertaining was enough to say no to the deal. But unfortunately once you sign you go and for me as crazy as it sounds I was up for the challenge. On top of that I had absolutely no desire to return to school for anything after my high school fiasco. So in October of 1991 I was off to boot camp in San Diego, California for a three month nightmare. It felt really cool leaving the airport in Indianapolis for San Diego. I was going away from home for the first time and other than going back to Texas, it was border line scary. But I was on my way and it did not take long at all to land in the back yard of san dog. So if leaving home was scary, try the confusion of arriving at our bus to take us to MCRD. Our bus driver was not even that mean or tough looking. I was beginning to think my recruiter, and the movie was not all true. Until that is we were picked up by our actual drill instructors. And that's when all hell broke loose and reality set in I was not in Kansas anymore Toto. When I was a boy I rarely finished anything that I started, but boot camp set the tone and was a real wake up call for me. Either you do or die there was no in between and no turning back, it was all or nothing. The Marine Corps taught me you go hard or you go home. This was not day care this was the Corp, hard core. But as much as the Marine Corps taught me how not to quit they still could not teach me how not to make unwise decisions. So about the latter part of my four year stint in the Corps I meet a girl and despite the advice I was giving by a buddy at the time, I married. At that moment my decision proved to be a fatal one as the success in my Marine Corps career would come crashing down. Years before marrying I worked hard to complete the difficult task of graduating boot camp with my mind somewhat still intact and in working order. I had survived the mental strain of the drill instructors, hand grenades, fifteen mile walks they called "humps" with thirty to forty pound gear on my back, and physical on top of physical training to come out as a Private First Class. A rank higher than one coming out of boot camp usually gets unless you were a squad leader or the guide, and I was neither. I was one of the recruits whose job was to keep the drill instructors house clean nothing meriting promotion out of boot camp. But I worked hard and as short as I was, especially for the "humps" I never gave up or gave them a hard time. Maybe that is what my drill instructors saw in me to warrant the promotion was that I had determination to succeed. A few years later after a tour in Japan and a few disappointing relationships I find myself up for another promotion and a new wife. The details of this marriage I will save for another work, but I will say it impacted my career as a Marine greatly. In fact the truth of the matter is that before I even married, my life was on a fault line and very unstable. The marriage was just the trigger to my already loaded gun. While I was in Japan it was the place to save money for a year. But I actually managed to spend most of my money on electronics, music, and on stuff that didn't even matter, instead of saving up for a down payment on a car or even a house. I was a product of bad decision making from the start. I grew up as the first born son and in my grandmother's eyes even though my dad had an older son, I was considered the first grandchild. So I was a spoiled little brat coming up and with my granny, what I wanted I usually got. Other family members might have been jealous of that, but that absolutely ruined me. Because what I got in material things I didn't get in how do I get these things for myself responsibly? In other words my financial life was screwed up before I even got my first job due to the lack of, you guessed it, a positive role model. And I missed that lesson in my schooling, because like I said I had my mind on other things. So I had a destiny to fail financially so to speak. By now you can start to see the foundation of my first marriages' failure, because indeed it had a lot to do with money and was built on a lie before love was even involved. Coming back from Japan was bitter sweet. I was glad to be back in my own country and yet I was disappointed in the amount of money that I could have saved but didn't. So while all of my piers were going to get cars I was playing loud music in my dorm and walking, it was not looking good for me at that point. It did not take me long to take what I did have and go car shopping. One day a buddy of mine and me set off one weekend to go and find each of us a car. We left off base on a bus, but we were determined to come back in our own ride. By the end of the day we had found what we had been looking for, at least my buddy did. He opted to go used and due to the spoil nature of my child hood I wanted to go new, and that is what I did. But because of my low down payment I could not get the new vehicle that I wanted so I had to settle for a Mitsubishi five speed truck. There were two problems with this, the first being it was not what I really wanted. And the second was I really did not know how to drive a five speed that well. Needless to say I got the truck and with the help of the California hills I learned how to drive that sucker really quick. Ok, the truck I had was really plain in every way and the big spender that I was I had to do something about it. But I was a low budget baller. So I did what I knew best and that was to spend money I didn't have. First thing I thought I had to do was to go and get me some of those wire rims that I saw on so many cars in Cali. The next thing a little system for the long rides and finally what good is a low rider truck without lowering it. This was finally my truck a brand new 1994 red custom Mitsubishi Might

Max. What a head turner and it also turned my wallet into empty. Not only did I have a truck payment I also had to make payments on the things I added to the truck itself. It did not leave me any room for movie money let alone a date at the end of the month. But I was styling and when I went back to Indiana on leave it attracted a lot of attention. What more could a twenty year old ask for at such a wise old age? The truck got the girls to look and then some I must add, but it left me empty and thinking I have to do something to make more money. Back in California I had a talk with a few of my fellow Marines about my financial struggle and they were telling me about how they plan to marry to receive more income. I must say the thought never crossed my mind, but it made sense. You get married in return you make more money in turn, you can move into housing and out of the bunk rooms, in return you have more bills. Oh wait more bills did I think of that? No of course not all I wanted was to be able to pay the ones I already had. So another wise decision had took place and set aside in the back of my mind once again. Now who would marry a short model type stud like me? And the fact that I was even considering was scary. My attempts to finding a girlfriend were even worse, until I stopped looking. And then one day while me and my buddy (the very one we bought cars together) was at the mall one day. His friend introduced me to her friend, we started dating, and it all became a part of history. Now this girl was my type light skin and thick with a thick accent. She threw me off which did not take much for me back then. But anyway we started kicking it and it turned out she already had a baby daughter that by the way did not bother me, because well I really liked both of them. What did bother me is what would my family think of me being with someone who already had a kid? And that was another problem, caring about what other people thought of me or how they saw me. It was a problem that I would not understand or even come to admit until years later. But I liked this girl so much that when we decided to marry each other we agreed to tell others, including my family, that her little girl was my own. Sure it would work she was only a baby and in my mind she looked like me, can't you tell? It was settled then we were getting married and everything was working out. But before I go there let me go back just a little. It also turns out that while I was dating this girl she also was dating someone else, and that in itself should have threw up a red flag, if I had my game face on. So I addressed the issue and she ended the relationship with the other guy. It was just a minor setback no big deal, right? Anyway time goes on and we are planning the wedding and she is planning to meet my dad's side of the family, because that's who was coming to dinner. They were coming to the wedding all the way from Texas to sunny California by plane. Not good if you knew the story of my granddad and his experience with flying. Anyway and mean while the preparation goes on and this is about the time another buddy of mine came to me and said, "Don't do it." The conversation went a little longer, but the bottom line was she was not the one for me. I took it that he and my other buddy knew more than I did about this girl or they were just looking out for me. Maybe it was both, either way in my stubbornness and my natural instinct to never back down from a fight, I didn't listen. It was going to go as planned. Now before the wedding I lived on base in dorms called barracks and I also had a roommate. He was cool at first, but then he started taking and using my stuff without permission and not putting it back. I did the civilized thing at first and talked to him about it and thought we had solved the problem. A few weeks to a month later we didn't. And we were back at the same problem that we were before, this time talk negotiations failed. This guy had the nerve to argue with me about my own stuff and it escalated into a beat down session on the spot. While the tussle assumed a corporal who lived next door broke us up. Well my roommate had a gun that he pulled out during the fight that he claimed he was just going to hit me with it. This would later come up in our court martial hearing that followed. Anyway long story short he ended up getting kicked out of the Marine Corps and up until then I was an outstanding Marine, other than my finances. So I was being demoted. But get this, because I was such an outstanding Marine, at the same time the Marine Corps was promoting me to Corporal. So instead of making Corporal and becoming a NCO (noncommissioned officer) I remained a Lance Corporal for another six months. I believe I set the record in being the fastest person to gain and lose rank in the Corps In the same day. My punishment besides loosing rank was barracks duty and confined to the barracks for a month. I consider I got off good, because I could have seen brig time over that stunt. If I had not been such a good Marine and if "Top" had not of served with me in Japan to put in a word for me, I probably would have been under the brig. After all of that garbage it was wedding time and one last attempt for my buddy and best man to talk me out of marrying the girl of my dreams. It didn't work and the wedding went on with my granddad taking that flight for my granny's sake despite his dislikes of it to San Diego. We did it up wedding dress limousine and all, what a beautiful day, or was it the beginning of a nightmare? Yes and yes. First thing was my family believed that my wife's daughter was mine and if they did not believe it, they never said anything, so that being the first lie past the test? Second the trouble I found myself in with losing rank before we got married was a clear sign of the trouble that was to come. Remember that nice low rider truck I put so much money into and one of the reasons I got married in the first place. It was the first victim of utter chaos in a long line of it. My wife and I had to be put on a waiting list for base housing so until we got it we had to move out in town. While we were out there my truck gained fans and it just happened to be car thieves.

One Friday night or Saturday morning depending on how you look at it, I came home from the club and parked my ride in its spot. Knowing that the same day I needed to go and get the alarm put on it, I took a nap. Yeah I know a nice truck in California with no alarm what was I thinking. Any who when I got up and was about to leave, my truck had already went, yes in a matter of hours my truck had been jacked. By the time the police was called and a report filed the only thing left behind was a pen and my truck being chopped and left for dead. All that was left was what I drove off the lot with minus everything I put into it. So it didn't have any rims or tires and I got rid of the originals, I decided to leave it where it was. I continued in a long streak of wise decisions and decided not to salvage the truck taking a huge investment loss. If you thought I had insurance then you thought wrong. Due to a financial difficulty, it was one of the things I let lapse and it ended up costing me big.

So now not only am I married living out in town with no vehicle, supposedly increasing cash flow. It begins going the exact opposite direction. Hey it's a good thing I am a Marine at this point, because nothing is going to hold me down, nothing. A little more time has gone by and we are finally on base and have a new ride thanks to my grandparents who helped me get a new toy in times of trouble. This time it was a 1989 (red) Camaro, and at what point in time does a person learn his lesson. I wanted to do the same thing that I did to the truck. Put rims and things on it that quite honestly was not a practical thing to do at the time. But it was something that I wanted to do and it was all about the attention. I managed to rustle up some rims for it and frankly, it was enough. That is all I had to put into it for a while, because even it started going south on me. Before anything else could happen to it besides attracting attention it started giving me trouble, electrical, ouch. But before it did that I had won tickets for a six month cruise on a ship with the US Navy. So I decided to take some leave before we got underway around the globe. My wife was pregnant and due any day with our first child and despite our misunderstandings we all took a two week journey back to Indiana and my home state of Texas. What I mean by "we" is my wife, little girl, and my pet Boa. That's right my snake, seems that somewhere I saw one wanted one and just had to have one of my own. So we went on our little happy vacation and arrived in Indiana with the snake, alive. I have no idea how I kept that snake, because my mom was not having it at all. In fact I was not staying in the house at all with that snake. Some things you just cannot remember. And what I did with the snake at that particular point in time was one of them. I believe a friend let me keep it at his house, but that is the best that I can do as far as memory goes.

Disaster Looming

Now my mom had never met my wife and this was the first she had ever heard of us being married, another ouch. If it was one person that was going to question whether or not if this little girl was mine, it was going to be my mom. And she did and despite what I said she knew that she was not mine, but she took her in eventually like I did. Oh well, water under the bridge. In the meantime while we were their traits I picked up from birth started kicking in. And while my wife who was about nine months pregnant at the time. All she could pretty much do was stay in bed while I went out clubbing with old high school friends. If that wasn't low enough in itself I ended up hooking up with a girl from the club and to impress her drove all the way to Chicago. Can you say what in the hell was I thinking? You don't have to because I was on a collision course to that very destination fast. I cannot speak for every man, but I am sure every man can relate when I say that. We will go out of our way to get some from the opposite sex most of the time. Anyway in the end we did not sleep together then, we just slept together if you know what I mean, but it was too late. I had made my mind up to that very occasion already anyway. So even though I did not carry it out physically at that time I had still cheated on my wife in my mind. And that sparked turmoil. After our journey through the mid-west and south we came back to Cali, moved into base housing, and I got ready to leave on a ship for the next six months. This was the time the mean little Camaro began to give me trouble. It would start in one place and not start in the other. That thing quickly lost its nice appeal and it goes to show you not everything that looks good is good for you. The upside to that was that our son, my first, was born and he was adorable. Not to mention that even though it was nasty I was still there for his birth and I got to cut his umbilical cord. Everything about that was cool except for the after birth, because it looked like an omelet gone badly. Oh well can't win them all, I was just thankful for a healthy little boy. The next stop was my six months pump.

The next few days was my wakeup call. I was about to leave my wife and two kids for six months to go on a trip around the world. It was exciting and scary at the same time on one hand I was about to see parts of the globe I had never seen before. And on the other hand I was leaving my family at the time for six whole months. The day arrived and my unit boarded the ship and by the end of the day we were sailing with the Navy on their gator class ships across the Pacific Ocean from San Diego. I must say it was pretty cool for a brief moment, because when that brief moment was gone we came across some rough seas battling waves that had to be more than thirty feet high and then some. I had never been sea sick on a boat before, but then again I had never been on a boat in the middle of the Pacific Ocean either. This was no ordinary boat, this was a gator class Navy ship called the Fort Fisher. And she held up on those treacherous Pacific Ocean waves, I on the other hand didn't. I had to get one of those sea sick patches from the doc in order to survive the storms. It took us about two weeks, but we finally made it to our first stop in the Hawaii islands. It was my first time being in Hawaii. The only drawback was that we were only there for a few days just to pick up supplies. So I did not get a chance to see much of the culture. It was still cool to see though. On our way on the tour I met my Navy counterpart in the ships Post Office. He and I would be in charge of the ships mail. He took care of the Navy side and well I took care of the Marine side. Oh yeah I was the Mail Man baby the 0161 United States Marine Corps Postal Clerk. And I must say it was a very rewarding position in the military especially on ship. If it was one thing that keeps moral up out in the middle of the ocean it was mail. We were like gods out on the water when it came to the sailors and marines and their families back home. We were the liaison to the family we had left behind. Fast forwarding through this trip was stops in Hong Kong, Singapore, Bahrain, Kenya, and one of my favorites, Australia I will tell you why shortly. Right now speaking of communication let's get back to life and our stop in Singapore. It was here I made a phone call home sometime in the afternoon Singapore time, but it was about three or four o'clock in the morning California time. I called home and some guy who was not supposed to be there answered our phone, do I need to say much more? So I tried to be nice and I asked him who he was and I need to speak to my wife. So when she got on the phone she said that he was a friend to one of her girlfriends who was spending the night. Ok, but this dude also had a friend of his own that was also staying with him in my house. Are you serious the longer the conversation went on the phone the hotter I got, because after all I may have made bad choices, but I was no dummy? It was at that moment that I knew exactly what was up in my own camp. I told my wife to put that dude back on the phone and then I told him to get out my house before I called the MP's back home to come put him out. I was hotter than fish grease and it took me a long time just to get over this guy answering my phone at three or four in the morning while I was gone. In fact it pretty much stayed with me the rest of the trip, let alone what they were more than likely doing there in the first place or even for how long, dang.

Oh well it was water under the bridge and there was nothing I could do about it at the time or could I? That brings me to my favorite stop of our six month pump, the land down under, Australia. This would be one stop that would be hard to forget, but it also made me forget about what had happened back home. Coming to port in Western Australia, Perth to be exact was an exciting feeling. Perth really reminded me of San Diego on the other side of the world. My postal buddy and I could not wait to get off ship and tour this foreign land. The first stop we made was a party that was just for us military personnel to welcome us to the land down under. It was great for a minute, but we did not want to spend our entire night in just one spot. So we started moving around to check out some spots and it didn't take long for some things to start checking us out. I quickly lost my buddy due to all of the attractions and met him back on the ship. To spare you of all the details in the week or so that we were in the port of Perth I had a brief encounter with a female on the beach and also pretty much moved in with another Australian woman at her place. That for some reason if I had not already been married would have married her. Back then I was such a confused one. She didn't know that and she also didn't know that

I was already married either. I wore no ring because I was too broke to afford one, oh yeah at this point I still had financial problems. The Australian woman didn't. I was becoming a global gigolo, not only did I have two relationships in Australia I had also had sexual relations with an African woman while in Mombasa, Kenya. In my sick and twisted mine I had felt redeemed about the troubles back home. And yet I still had to face them once I got back, which was now time. After six months the Exxex group was pulling back into the Coronado bay of San Diego, what a trip. It was time to face the music. And when we were finally debriefed and back home I greeted my wife and two kids as if nothing ever happened. But deep down inside I knew and she knew that things had changed and a lot of things were wrong. We were just glad to see each other despite the circumstances, even if our relationship was built on a lie that was growing bigger every day.

So as time went on the Australian woman and other women I met would keep in touch while my wife and I grew farther apart. One day we got into an argument so bad that we could no longer hide our misguided marriage. At one point in time I had said to myself that I would never beat a woman like my dad did with my mom. One of the main reasons they got a divorce in the first place. The other, well he was a gigolo too. Anyway my wife and I had a disagreement and at this point have no idea what it was about. All I know is that I was tired of fighting and just wanted to leave the house. She was not having it and while I was trying to get out she was pulling on my clothes to keep me in. That was not a good idea, because in a split second and before I knew it I was throwing a stack of magazines at her and saying would you just let me go. The next thing I know she is leaving with the kids just walking down the street crying; a mistake none the less while living on base. Well, while walking the Military Police saw her strolling down the street with the kids crying and asked her what was wrong. She told them we had a fight (in reality it was an argument) but that was enough for them to come and arrest me for family violence. And it was also enough for the word to go out to my unit. Here I am detained until my Sargent could come and pick me up from the brig until this situation could get straightened out. In the end my wife never officially filed charges, because it really wasn't anything but a big misunderstanding. We did have to go to counseling though, did it work? Let's just say we were past counseling. The very long distant relationships had to stop and I had to get real about life. That is what we tried to do together and I was coming to the end of my tour in the Marine Corps real fast. I wanted to stay in the Corps and I had talked to my step brother who was also in out in Georgia at an air wing station. This was the place I wanted to go and this is what I asked of the Marine Corps, but with so many problems I was facing with the last half of my four year term. I was like if they could not guarantee me a transfer to an air wing station in Georgia, there was no guarantee that I was going to stay in. And they couldn't, so I didn't stay, another wise decision by a true scholar such as me.

I also thought by getting out would help our situation. I also thought that by moving from California back to Texas would also improve drama. I was wrong on both counts, because we did both of those things and both failed. I got out of the military and we moved in with my dad back in Texas until we could find a place. I don't even believe it lasted a month, because I had to find work and a place to stay. And with my wife missing her mom back in Cali both of our attitudes and temper was causing major drama. One day while we were going through all of this drama arguing and such, I received a phone call from an old friend. It happened to be the girl I met at a club while home on leave. The one I drove to Chicago just because, and only I could make a bad situation worse. At this point in time I began talking to her while my wife and I were arguing. I was pretending like nothing was wrong, asking her how she was doing, and that I remembered her and on and on. Though I could not hear her very well due to the yelling, I asked her if I could call her back, got her number and that was that. A little time went by and my wife decided she had enough. She told me she was going back to California and that if I wanted to see her or the kids again I would have to go too. With my big ego, that was not happening, and I made plans of my own. So with all of our stuff in storage, my wife took the kids and hopped on the next bus smoking back to Oceanside, California. I on the other hand jumped in my grandpa's old Cadillac that I inquired from his estate after he died. Then I headed back to Indiana where my mom, my brothers, my grandma, and that female that I was talking to were waiting. Leaving my past four years of the Marine Corps behind me was what I was trying to do; an experience that turned really bad due only to the bad choices that I was making and continuing to make. Digging deeper let's see what else we can turn up. By now my wife was settled back in Cali and I was back in Indiana. It was just about winter and getting cold. Meanwhile I hooked back up with a buddy of mine from high school and we started hanging out again. I ended up taking a trip to see no other than the girl I met while home on leave to finish what we started years ago. We became real good friends in fact it grew into a relationship fast, probably too fast. The night my mom came in the room and saw us getting busy in my brothers bunk bed, would have been a good sign that I was in danger Will Robinson. My boy had got me a job where he was working at and then we decided to share an apartment. Believe it or not at about twenty four years old, this would be my introduction into smoking weed, and what an introduction. My boy and I were watching Friday a movie I had never seen before; as much as I had never smoked weed before, the combination was hilarious. In which without a doubt had me hooked to the feeling. From that point on not only was I prone to making bad decisions I was now making them under the influence of narcotics. I—was—in—trouble. The job we had was going alright and between my buddy and me we kept the lights on. About this time this is where things started getting interesting. On the weekends I would run over to Lafayette and pick up my main squeeze at the time and we would spend the weekend together. This main squeeze would be in fact no doubt the girl I had very reason to come back to Indiana in the first place. The one who called me while I was still in the Lone Star state of Texas, who, had power over me. Anyway this would be just about an every weekend thing and while my buddy was smashing on his girl I was no doubt having fun with mine. It turns out I was having too much fun and she became pregnant. Now this was how bright I was. I had found out that this girl was still in high school and yet that was too late, because

I continued to see her and now she was pregnant. I was absolutely a piece of work. And if the law had found out then I would have been thrown under the jail. But we had a plain and this was our plan. We would ask her mom if I could move in with them so I could find a job in Lafayette. This was in order to take care of her daughter. I am laughing out loud writing this while remembering the day. I couldn't even take care of myself and I wanted to take care of someone else. It was just a ridiculous idea that happened to work, because that is exactly what happened. And I left a friend of many years behind stuck with all the bills in an apartment we shared. I did all of this for a girl I knew for less than a year, and I didn't even discuss it with him first. Another wise decision from the scholar fueled only by my little head. Just before all of this happened I received a phone call from my wife; yes I was still legally married. And we began arguing over the phone she wanted me to come back to California. Considering all of the things that we went through out there, my heart was not in it and I was in too deep with my current situation. This would be the last I would here from her for a very long time, because I refused to go back. At this point in time I needed and everyone else around me needed some serious boots. I was a danger to myself and everyone around me. All it would take was something to trigger the hidden volcano. Little did I know that device was right up the road and right with me? I landed several good jobs in Lafayette; one at Wabash National and the other at the Subaru plant. Probably two of the best jobs in Indiana period and I managed to mess both of them up. Due to my once again troubled relationship with a female who did not even know how to get her own life together; much less mine and my wise choices in life. Over time I would have a beautiful son with this girl, get and lose two good jobs, get evicted from our apartment, and she and her mom would kick me out of their house more than once. Which by the way you would think would be the end of the drama, but it wasn't. In between all of that my girlfriend's mom at the time would help us out after my old caddie stopped running by co-signing on a car for us. As if I could not add to the current situation by going deeper into debt not only by money, but personal as well. It was all based on a bad personal decision at the time that I thought was a good one. After all I was a twenty something year old kid involved with a high school student; and I don't believe she ever graduated high school I don't remember. But what I do remember is that she got an apartment and I moved in with her and my son, another mistake by the all-time master of them all. Fast forwarding it didn't take long for us to bump heads. And I found myself moving back in with my mom in old Logansport, Indiana. Now I find myself back on the dating seen; and not only was I sleeping with my ex-girlfriends friend I was hooking up with a friend of hers. It was absolutely ludicrous and I was in the middle of a dream/nightmare. This is how this played out there is no way to get around this story without a little more detail than what I want to tell, so here we go. After I slept with my ex-girlfriends friend she in return hooked me up with a friend of hers. And in that instance we began seeing and sleeping with each other. This is where I have to say that all of this happened so fast it is making my head spin to this very day. Not to mention that I am trying to keep all of these names out even fake ones, because that would even confuse me more.

Pimping is not easy

One night the current girlfriend I had at the time decided to stop by her friend's house; yes the one who hooked me up with her, and the one I had relations with. Anyway my son's mom stops by and immediately she began arguing with me about us being there. She wanted us to leave, but I told her we had every right to be there as she did. It went on and on and as stubborn as I was instead of taking our party somewhere else, I argued with a woman. I was tired of her invading my personal space and in my anger I grabbed her by the throat to push her away. I told her that she needed to stay out of my face and that I never wanted to see her again. While that no doubt made her leave it also made her go to the cops, because the next thing I know Johnny law is contacting me telling me that she is pressing charges. And they have pictures of her neck which was proof that I beat her. I just keep finding myself deeper in trouble and it was becoming a house hold name for me. They didn't arrest me, but I had to go to court, take anger management classes, and do community service. Not to mention I had a restraining order in affect for I can't even remember how long. All I know it was for a long time. I did what the courts had inquired of me and was just about to finish up anger management class. And then for some ungodly reason I ended up moving back in with none other than my son's mom. The very person who got the police to hand me a battery charge and a restraining order was asking me back, was it love or stupidity? In my case it was probably more the latter. Ok, so now in between my son's mom asking me back; knowing that she knew I had cheated on her and she had cheated on me. I was leaving this other relationship with a seed planted in her-which by the way I did not know until years later. Back to my son's mom, I am once again back in her apartment after being kicked out I don't know how many times and this time with a restraining order hanging over my head. But you don't think about that when you got your little head thinking for you or you have a son to look after. And besides that by this time this girl and I would have serious history together. I mean I can remember one time while we were apart and I was staying with my mom. I did one of the dumbest things you don't even see in reality shows today. I mean while we are trying to work things out and we were apart, deep down inside I had a feeling that she was still playing on me. So while she was staying at a friend's talking to me on the phone all of a sudden she had to go, but when I offered to come and see her and my son she said no. I went into overdrive. I tried to sneak my mom's car and drive all the way to Lafayette, but she wasn't having that. Then I tried asking and that didn't work either, I was hot I had no other choice. I started walking I was determined to find out what she was doing. How determined? Lafayette was close to forty miles from Logansport and it was in the middle of winter with snow on the ground, that's how much? Needless to say I made it after a real nice guy offered to give me a ride out of the kindness of his heart, especially after I told him why. This was just one of the craziest things; other than just being with her that I did with and for this girl.

So here I am back at her apartment. This would be for the last time, because I have a restraining order and for some reason after some time pass we get into another argument. So the first thing she wants to do after she told me to leave, and I was not about to go this time, was to call the law. Now I had already at one time plotted to push her out of a moving car one day while we were arguing driving down the highway. That was just how fried my mind was. This time I was done. I was not going to go to jail for being in a place I was not supposed to be. And I was not going back to my mom's house either. My only option was to leave and not come back. So I loaded up the car with what I could carry and with no place to go, I drove to Indianapolis. This was the beginning of the end. Within three years of being back in Indiana I managed to get into a relationship with a girl who was still in high school while I was still married, and ditch a friend in an apartment we got together for this girl. I had sex with her friend and then I ended up being with the girl's friend that I had sex with. I started experimenting with drugs and I also developed a police record. I helped pull off a talent show and I also managed to help another girl that I had a relationship with escape from the law. I managed to get my driver's license revoked and suspended and because I had music talent along with another friend of mine was about to head to MTV. Until, that is I had no choice but to leave which brought me to Indianapolis. It is here that I took my drug abuse to the next level. While I was looking for work at a work today get paid today agency I met a guy who seemed to have his act together and let me just reiterate seemed to have it together. I followed this guy like a little lost puppy. Because let's face it I was just like a little lost puppy without a home. I was in a city I knew very little about except how to get to a couple of malls. I had very little cash and no place to lay my head for a good night rest. So I became this guy's chauffeur and in return he let me stay where he stayed in a motel. While staying with him I found out that he had come into some money from some type of settlement. It didn't take me long to find out that he was also a crack head. And that is exactly what he started using that money for. All of a sudden dealers started knocking at the door and of course when you have drugs you have an entourage. So along with the drugs came company in the female kind.

Drug Abuse

This is where I met my next two associates. One of them would let me become her roommate for the next month or so. This would be a ride I will never forget, let's go. The crack head I was giving rides for started wigging out after a couple of days of being strung out. Then he started flipping on me. So with nowhere to go again, I thought it would be best that I left before me or he found our self-dead. I talked to the girls that would come by and get hits off of this guy and one of them agreed to let me stay with her. I thought that was cool, because she didn't know me from Adam and she was letting me become her roommate. My new roommate had a house just on the eastside of downtown Indianapolis. She shared this place with her little girl. Her friend that came with her to the motel room would also stay there a lot, and it would turn out this little beauty had a thing for me. Uh oh was it trouble brewing in the air? Everywhere I went it was close behind me like stink on crap. Anyway more on that in a minute, let's see what happened after I moved in. It wasn't long before I started meeting new people. One person I will never forget just happened to be, you guessed it, another drug dealer. He took an interest in me real quick it seems that I had what he needed. A set of wheels and as long as I could come he could have them. I was up for an adventure. I started riding around with him and a buddy of his while they did their thing selling dope. While sitting in the back seat I started learning the game on the cool. How he picked up, where he picked up and I already knew the size of a rock. I just had to get my weights down and I was going to put myself on, or so I thought. Anyway being that I always had a positive role model in my life I tried to learn everything from this guy and his friend. They even claimed that they were GD and that is what I wanted to claim too, because that is how I thought you got love in the street. For most people on the street this was their way of thinking as well; join a gang get respect and love. A gang was your protection on the street homie, was I ever wrong about that one. I went to this guy's house, I met his mom, and I saw a few of his connects. We ate together even saw a few drama scenes together. One drama scene was dealing with shooting guns and another about to shoot down somebody. All in a day's work of a street thug I suppose. Well it did not take long for this guy to start tripping on me too. I guess I was getting to close and or he wanted the car for himself, because one day he dropped me off and I did not see him for a long time. So here I am back at the house chilling with these females getting high and having the time of our lives. I was ready to try out what I had learned in the street and step into my new occupation of becoming a drug dealer. At the ripe young age of about only twenty-six, it must have been the right time. I was about to step into the big leagues. But first I had to deal with my roommate's friend who had her eye on me. One day I went with her back to her spot so she could get cleaned up and grab some more clothes. With my mind somewhere else like making some money little did I know she was taking me back to her spot so she could smash. I think I knew a little bit after a minute. Even though she was fine something did not seem right about her. And everything in me was telling me don't go through with it, so I didn't. I had one more chance on a different day when we went to get high together up stairs, but I couldn't do it. After that the real she came out of nowhere one day. And I became her enemy all of a sudden. Then she threatened to call her brother or some killer she knew to take care of me. I was like dang here we go. After she tried to kick my tail, she was going to get somebody to kick my tail. Or worse kill me at least that is what she said anyway. People will say anything while pissed off. First thought in my mind was that she was pissed off because I didn't have sex with her. The second thought was I needed to get a gun to defend myself. I am so glad that things cooled off and I did not have to take it there, but it was quite funny after the fact.

Now I was ready to get my work on and it just so happened that my roommate's boyfriend had recently got out of jail. He was the brother of a king pin who specialized in selling none other than crack. I had a plan of course, and of course he did too. One night we were up in the room getting high and I asked him to put me on with some of his stuff. So I traded him a bag of crack for most of my music gear, everything except for my drum machine. I had to get on and start making some money, because I was dead broke and I needed to come up fast. He started telling me about the game. And how you should test your product before you sell it so that you will know what you would be selling. He convinced me to try some crack and it was like getting high off weed with three types of steroids built in. It was like a super high with a super-fast kick, and I wanted more. I began smoking so much crack that finally I just walked off so I could just go sit down somewhere. I found out real quick that this was not like smoking weed. And while I was walking downstairs I could hear voices laughing and talking in my ear. I turned around like what did you say, but nothing was there. I finally got to the couch to lie down. My heart was beating so hard and fast that even though I did not know Him. I asked God that if He would let me live, I would never smoke crack ever again. The next day came and I woke up. I never smoked another crack rock again. But as crazy as it sounds it didn't stop me from wanting to sell it though. I was still out there and it was going to take me just a little bit more for me to come back home. In the meantime I met my roommate's mom, her brother and his girlfriend and they were real cool people. I mean I was a stranger from out of town and they allowed me to spend the holidays with them. How cool was that? I thought it was very cool, but it wasn't long after that my brother who stayed in Indianapolis got in touch with my mom. It wasn't long before she found me and convinced me to go back to Texas to live with my dad. Something that I didn't really want to do, but she said do it for her, because she feared that I was going to die in the streets of Indianapolis. So I called my dad and asked him if I could come back to live with him. He said he wouldn't mind only if I was straight. Of course I thought he was talking about if I was gay or not and I told him I liked women. He said, "No I mean are you on drugs?" And of course I lied, because I knew my mom wanted me off those streets. And he would not let me if he knew I was smoking weed. Even though I found out he used to smoke weed when he was my age or younger. But anyway before I could leave Indianapolis I had to find out where my car was (laughing out loud) that is so sad. I called the guy who had it and told him I needed it back, but he never brought it. So I had to use drastic measures and I got in-touch with his mom, told her the story, and she tracked him down so I could get my car. At the end of the day and out of fear of me turning him and his operation in to the cops, the car showed up in a car pound. It needed a lot of work so I decided just to leave it and head back to Texas. Of course there is more to this story like any other story, but because it happened so fast and I was getting so high, the details remain juggling in my head. It's time to get into the meat and potatoes of my journey. The move back to my home state of Texas would be my final destination before freedom.

On My Way Home

As soon as I arrived back in Sweetwater I didn't waste any time looking for a job. It was not only because I needed it, but it would also keep my dad and my step mom off of my back. It was around 1998 and here I am about twenty-six years old back at home living with my dad acting like I was still a teenager. If I was looking at my situation like, 'what the hell' you know how they could have seen it a lot worse than I did. I was past time of I really did not care and total self-destruction. Anyone who was around me I was going to take with me in some form or fashion, so I thought. I landed a cool job with a temp agency. All it required was for me to sit on a panel during a court trial to help make a decision in a court case.

How cool is that and it paid ten dollars an hour just to sit, take notes, and give your opinion. Not a bad gig, it just didn't last. I had the opportunity to stay on with the temp company. All I had to do was just take a drug test. Would I pass it? Unfortunately not, I was too busy trying to get high and ruined any chances of me getting on permanently with this company. Any attempts to clean my system out failed obviously, because I was back where I started, jobless looking for work. I believe the only work I was looking to do was what was familiar, to get my hustle on. One day I was at my cousin's house and she was talking to an old friend from way back on Hughes Street, grade school, and high school days before we moved away. He was in town from Dallas, we hooked back up and did just that, got our hustle on. He had a "connect" in Dallas where he could score a pound of weed. We probably would have got more if I had the money, but I pitched in what I had and we did what we had to do. After we got what we needed we headed back to the water to get the word out. And of course it didn't take long for it to fire up. I was in it to make a little money at first, but my boy he had other plans, plans that I really wasn't down with at first after my Indianapolis episode. Somehow it did not take me long to change that up and our friendship, due to none other than a female. While we were out doing our thing we managed to slip away and have a little fun. We posted up one night at this club. At the time the only real hot spot in Sweetwater as far as clubs was concerned. This place was to get our drink on and to see what we could get into. Little did either one of us know that this night would be one of our last nights as a dynamic duo. While I was minding my business as we mingled in the crowd he spots a fine sister in the hallway of the club. And of course the deal was if you spot her you got her, no problem for me. But while he was trying to get this girls attention she kept trying to get mine. And in my mind the way she kept cutting at me with those pretty hazel eyes, I was going to make that move and I told him so. The next thing you know we started talking after the club. We talked about going to the café for the after party and while there I decided I didn't need anybody else, but her. One thing led to another and the next thing you know we were making plans to call and see each other again like two high school sweethearts. Little did I know at the time that she was still in high school as a senior? When I did find out it was too late, I was in it to win it. She was going to be "My Boo". She was Bonnie to my Clyde you get the point. I didn't care if she was still in school and it turns out she was down for whatever, my kind of girl. This is just how sick and twisted my mind had become. I had dinner reservations with the devil every night and he came looking for me whenever I didn't show up. It would start out that I would talk to this girl on the phone. But it didn't take me long for me to start going back to my old stomping grounds in the projects on Hughes Street to see her. By this time I met her mom, her cousins, and I even found out that one of her cousins was my cousin. But the real freaky catch to all of this was that her granddad and grandma use to take her over to my grandpa's house when she was just a little girl, and we just happen to be over there at the time. The very thing I remember the most was those eyes; it took me a minute, but it was more to this than just those eyes. It did not take us long to hit it off and start seeing each other on a regular basis. In fact it was not long at all before I was moving in and claiming territory like the lion I never knew I was. She liked to smoke weed, I like to smoke weed, we all liked to smoke weed. Anyway I had landed a job at the local supermarket as a stocker not only for some income, but to support our habit. It didn't take a rocket scientist to know that it wasn't going to be enough. Now her mother turns out smoked a little bit more than just weed, she was on the hard stuff. The very same stuff I vowed I would never smoke again, but she also sold it for a little extra cash. With that we had a connection in the game. This is how we were going to come up at least this is what I thought. We made a few runs, did a few deals, sold some product, and was moving our way up. It was just not fast enough in this little town. We had to step the game up and go outside Nolan County. The thing is our hustle was being hated on by many and it didn't take long to figure this one out. We were set up to make an out-of-town deal. That same deal eventually went bad. This was not the only time we got took by some crack heads, in fact, that's just how it was in the game. But it was more to it than that with me. This whole time we were doing our thing together I was starting to change. It just didn't feel right to me anymore. At one time I was going for kingpin status, and the next moment I was moving toward getting out. Something was happening to me from the inside where nobody could see. Months went by and while we were checking out the block watching these other guys get their hustle on. All I could think about was that they were doing it all wrong and just making the block hot. Selling to anyone just to make a buck was not cool and all it did was draw attention to you. Anyway it did not take me long to seclude myself from everyone else. Maybe they thought I was too good for them, but the truth was I was just changing.

And my desire to remain in the game was slowly leaving. At this point the job at the supermarket continued, the relationship with my girl was going strong. Then I started picking up a hobby I had not done in years, I started drawing again. The store had cardboard boxes that come off the trucks and I saved some, because I thought it would be pretty cool as a canvas. It turns out that it was. I drew a blue and green low rider truck that made headlines as far as I was concerned. It was drawn on cardboard using a pen and map colors. Then my cousin's husband took it and outlined it with a fine black marker and made it pop. I showed a few people and even got a few orders in to draw for others like a business. But it was a conflict of interest and too time consuming. Long story short it was too much work and the pay did not come fast enough. So it faded away quick as far as the business side of it was concerned, but I still managed to get high and draw. It was like a release from the grind. My girl and I was still doing our thing, but it was just not working out the same. It even came down to the point where I talked to her and was like we need to do something different, something does not seem right. It was like all of a sudden I lost interest in selling dope. I was beginning to wonder what the hell was wrong.

A New Course

I had another cousin who was around my middle brother's age who came to see me one day when I was in the middle of my grind movement. He grew up in the same area in fact he lived right up the street as kids. Anyway he was now living his life for God. One day he stopped by took out some oil and put it on my head and prayed for me. I didn't know anything about what he just did, but I tell you it was not long after that that my whole demeanor changed. Looking back, what he did was an act to steer me heading a different direction than where I was going before. One thing was for sure I was looking at my situation in a whole different way. And now I was looking for a way out even while we were still pushing. One early summer day while we were out doing the same old same old, word got back that a friend from around the way had got stopped by the police. In his possession he had rock cocaine. This was not good, because not only did he have crack in his car, but he was also stopped in a school zone which by the way seemed to be a set up from the start. But that was just the way my brain worked and it does not make a difference now. What was different was me. And after all that went down I became even more cautious. Did he talk on the inside or what? It was just a thought that ran through my head as a dealer on the street. That too does not make a difference. What was different was me.

So we slowly but surely discontinued or reign of drug trafficking and continued our other bad habit of weed smoking. My girl's mom was still smoking crack; not sure at this time if she was still selling. But I had made it clear that we should stop. This was due to the heat that was turning up everywhere. I knew we had to move around and it had to be soon. We had already tried once moving in with someone else, but that did not last long. So we took another approach and my girl applied for housing after she graduated high school. As crazy as the idea was it was our only option, and she got it. Just over eleven years to the day I was living back in the same projects I once lived in as a kid after the tornado in 1986, Circle Drive. In the meantime my son from Indiana was allowed to come live with me for a little while and like everything else at the time I took his visit for granted. Even though we were not selling crack anymore we still got high on a daily basis. My son was caught right in the middle of the selfish acts of abuse.

CHAPTER 2

The Beginning

It was not long after we moved to Circle Drive that one of our worst fears had come to past. It seemed that the law enforcement agency launched a city wide drug bust, and they hit hard. Everywhere activity had been was hit by task force including yours truly, Bonny and Clyde's last known location. And it was also concluded that my girlfriend's mom had been caught up in the drama as well. At this point in time my gut feeling served me well in getting out when we did. If we had not, we would have been looking at close to life in jail in the direction we were going. After this, things just started going downhill more and more. I really loved my girl at the time. And even though she knew I was still legally married. She was willing to go the extra mile with me in order for me to get a divorce so that we could get married. Unfortunately, that was also nipped in the bud after I flipped the script and became willing to cheat on her with someone from my job. I even questioned my own insanity at this point. I had the girl of my dreams. To me she was one of the finest girls in Sweetwater. She was the glove to my hand and yet we started falling apart. In fact everything started to fall apart, what in the hell was wrong with me? I was absolutely losing my mind. And I felt like everything around me was crushing my very existence. I did not want to go out to the clubs or café anymore, I did not even want to hang around the same people anymore. I lost interest in everything. I instantly began feeling like how I treated a lot of people including myself, like dirt. Then I lost interest in alcohol, it started tasting like urine to me. Then I treated smoking cigarettes like what it caused and started throwing them out. It seemed like everything that was bringing me comfort was not doing it anymore, including getting along with my girl. It seemed like I would just find something to get into it with her to cause some kind of commotion. Finally one day in the early months of the year 2000 I could not take myself any longer. I had reached a point of complete limbo. I could not go forward and I could not go back. I felt everyone was against me and I was for no one. After I had an argument with my girl I went for a drive and began contemplating my life. Since I was never fond of taking my own life I pulled to the side of the road down the street from my auntie's house, parked the car and began to cry. For the first time in my life my past finally caught up with my present and I was dwelling on it. While I sat there in my car crying something in me directed me to go to my aunt's house. And after a moment that is exactly where I went. Living with my aunt was her daughter, my cousin's mom. The same cousin who came and prayed for me that day, anyway she was also my cousin and she had a relationship with God as well. So much so that she was always trying to get us to see Him how she saw Him, and to be honest it was a turn off to say the least. Never the less this was one time I felt compelled to go and have a chat with my cousin. So we just started having a normal conversation at first, but the way she was looking at me she could tell that this was but a normal conversation. She started asking me was I alright and at that moment in time I broke down without hesitation. I could not hold my feelings inside any longer. She knew I needed help, she also knew what I needed to do. And on top of that, she also knew it was time. Time for me to give my life back to the one who created me and that is exactly what I did. Crying and all, I said the sinner's prayer and accepted Jesus in my life. In the midst of saying it a miracle was beginning to happen inside of me. It felt like everything that I had lived for to that day was lifted off of me, and I became a brand new being. My past life and world felt like it had been completely erased from memory. I tried going back to my girl and doing the same thing; mainly smoking weed, and I just could not do it anymore. Something in me completely denounced it; it even smelled like garbage to me. And to my amazement, that was something that I thought I would never stop doing. I absolutely thought I had to have weed to fuel my imagination and get me by. It was no longer working out that way in fact staying with my girlfriend was not working anymore either. So I packed my clothes and had her drop me off at my aunt's house leaving her with everything, which at this time was not much at all. I instead immediately wanted to know who this was that changed in an instant my perspective on life. My cousin told me the first thing that I needed was a bible. In the meantime I began reading one of hers. But after staying with my aunt and cousin for a little bit, I had told my dad that I gave my life to God. And he allowed me to move back into his house for a while. He also let me use one of his bibles until I could get my own.

In which my step mom and my cousin wanted to get one for me, but I could not wait I had to read about this God who did such a radical change in me. Who was He? I dove into the Holy Bible like a diver ready to get into the ocean, hard and fast. I started reading in Proverbs and Job, but my cousin told that I should start reading in the New Testament. Because that was the life of Jesus and was the very reason I come into a relationship with God in the first place. So I changed gears. And after I received my own bible from my step mom I began reading the New Testament. I was amazed at what Jesus Christ went through here on earth.

Beginning Faith Walk

I tried to share the good news with my girlfriend and indeed gave her a chance to have the same relationship with God, just like I had come into one with Him. She attended a church service with me and I even bought her a bible, but it turned out that she did not want anything to do with God. She only did it to hold on to what we had in the past and the Lord knew, because He spoke that very thing through the pastor of the church. I was to let go of her she was not the one for me. It was not long after that we became just friends and even that was a hindrance. By now I was having quite a few debates and discussions with my step mom dealing with scriptures. And it was apparent that my view of a relationship with God and hers was quite different. Though I never doubted that she did not have a relationship with the Lord, I just believed it was based more on religion than a relationship. And with that said it was a big difference between the two. We had several conversations from time to time and some of them, because of my zeal for God, became quite heated. I have no doubt that she went back to my dad about some of them, because one day he came at me in the most unusual way about Gods Word and it was very dramatic. I don't remember the topic, but I do remember him saying that whatever it was I was reading in the bible, it was not in there, and that I was not reading it right. However that which I was reading was word for word straight from the book and I believed it to be true. At that moment he became so angry at me that he told me I had to get out of his house and I had to live somewhere else. And to make sure I was going to go he called his reverend at his church at the time to make sure that I did just that. Through all of this I knew the hand of God was upon me, because though it was chaotic I was calm and I believed in God. It seemed the very sword I was given by my step mom was the very sword that triggered chaos between us all. Let me tell you why I had such faith in God in time of such a chaotic moment. Before my dad kicked me out of his house one night and before I went to sleep. I prayed and asked the Lord to heal my body. In return I told Him that I would go and say and do whatever He wanted me too if He did. The next morning I was healed. See my past was living in me in the form of some type of disease. And I was too scared to go get checked out to see what it was. But I knew it was something serious because my body did not feel right. And I had a bump or something near my groan, on top of that I always felt tired. In my quest to not care so much about whom I had sex with and without a condom, I just knew it had to do with something sexually. It was not the first time that I contracted a sexual transmitted disease, but it was the first time that it did not burn while I had it. So I did not know what it was or even how long it had been there. All I know is that I did not feel right. So that night when I asked God to heal me in faith and I woke up the next morning looking down at my groan with that lump gone, I felt like a new person. I knew that God was God and that my question that rattled the back of my mind in early childhood years was being answered. "Who made us and how did we get here?" In my mind it was He Who healed me and that He created all we are, and I just believed.

Being kicked out of my dad's house was God's will for me. He allowed me to see my dad for who he really was, and this was only the beginning. I called my cousin to see if she could come and get me and my aunt let me stay with them again. But I had to go, God had plans for me that I was about to find out about. My cousin told me I needed to get a hold of my mom and brother so I could go and stay with them. After I received my last check from my supermarket job, I bought a bus ticket and headed for Columbus Ohio. It was in Columbus that I saw my first concert. An outside event of the Gospel Gangsta's a Christian rap group that was one of my favorites at the time. It was around the summer of 2000 about a few months after I first got saved. And while I enjoyed the event I also was trying to figure out what God's will was for me. So I stuck around after the show and got to meet the group. I got a poster and they all signed it. I knew that one of the members of the group, "Chilly" made most, if not all of their beats and I also made beats. So being a new Christian I naturally assumed that this must be God's will for me to go with these guys and make music. I would be wrong, I talked with Chilly and he gave me his pager number at the time and told me to send him some tracks. Another member of the group just looked at me and gave me a hug. But I was not going with the group this was not God's will for me. Disappointed and relieved at the same time I moved on and waited for my brother to come pick me up from the event. While I was waiting a guy offered me a button that simply said "Walking Faith." I didn't have any money, but then he said "this looks like you" and he gave it to me. From that day on I knew that there was going to be more to this journey than just joining a Christian rap group. I still had a lot to learn about myself and God. In other words I had a lot of growing to do.

Now my brother only lived in a one bedroom apartment outside of Columbus, and since my mom lived with him too, there was not much room for me to stay there. So they took me downtown and I got a room at the YMCA men's shelter. Here I got a job with a window cleaning company to pay for my stay and it allowed me to continue to read the bible. Every chance I got I was reading about what the Lord had to say about His people and to His people. The more I read the more amazed I became and it was evident that God was no joke. One day God revealed to me that He wanted me to go to a church in Columbus. So I went to one I had seen on TV. And while there I felt the presence of God in that place like I had never felt before, even when I got saved. It was like a constant pressure all around me engulfing me like an invisible force field. All I could do was raise my hands and cry out like many times I did before after I kneeled down to pray or praise God. It was absolutely an overwhelming experience that caused me to think about nothing else. After the service I went back to my room and I continued to read and read some more. I went through the entire summer working at the window cleaning company and reading the Word of the Lord. At the same time I was writing and calling the girl I still considered to be my girlfriend, who at the time was still being a hindrance to my relationship with God, even a thousand miles away. One day I just stopped receiving calls and letters. So I called to check up on her. After all at the time she was the love of my life, and she was hard to let go. I got a hold of her and she said that she was alright, but I could tell in her voice that something was wrong. After I got off of the phone with her I could feel in my heart that she had moved on, it was just no real proof at the time. In the mean time I kept going, pushing, moving closer to God learning more about Him. It seemed that I had developed an overwhelming desire to be consumed with the presence of God. One day towards the end of the summer the Lord spoke to my heart and told me it was time to move on from the YMCA and leave my present job. I obeyed and moved back in with my brother thinking that the Lord was only going to keep me there only for a short time, and He did, it was just not in the way that I thought. My brother let me come back to his small apartment, because he thought I would not be there for a long time, and I told him that because that is what I believed. But those who believe in God know or should know that God never works in a way that we can figure out what is going to happen next.

The week or so that I thought I would be at my brothers apartment turned into weeks, then months. I quickly found myself without any money and wondering what was going on. After a while my brother started getting agitated at me about being in his space, I can't say that I didn't blame him. It was now September 2000 and my brother received a call from my granny and my dad that my granddad had died. I did not even have the courage to get on the phone to talk to either one of them, because I knew I did not have the heart to go to the funeral or the money to get there. I am sure they would have paid my way back home if they knew my situation. But my heart ached and I didn't have the courage to go. I asked my brother if he was going to go and he said, "No" and I didn't have any peace about going myself. I must be honest here. I was not a big fan of my granddad and that had built up over many years, starting with my child hood and adolescent years. Don't get it twisted or anything I am sure my granddad loved me in his own way, it was just not in a way that I liked. Take for instance one day when I lived with my dad my sophomore year of high school. My dad wanted me to go to church, but I did not want to go that day. And when he forced me to go it made me very upset. This was not the only time my dad went off because of not wanting to go to church with him. He once started beating my mom after she spoke for my brothers and me for not wanting to go to church with him. I was eleven or twelve then and I wanted to kill my dad for that. If he had not of left he would have felt the knife I had from the kitchen. But instead I took out my anger on his hat that he dropped during his brawl with mom. So back to the year 1988 we got into it and I eventually made a B line out the patio door tearing down the screen while at it. In the end he caught me but I tried anyway to leave. Well my dad told my granddad and then he took me over to their house. While I was there I did not say much to him. He just continued to tell me I was never going to amount to anything and that I was disrespecting him and my dad. I just looked him in the eye. And I will never forget that while I did that, he popped me in the back of my head. And he told me that I was not going to disrespect him or my dad again, and for me to stick my lips back in. He continued to say "after all he had did for us" meaning me and my brothers. I found out later in life money can't buy you love. A big lesson I had to learn the hard way. After he had said and did that it really made me resent him and I never looked at him the same again. So even though I was sad of his passing and I loved him, I loved God more and was willing to do His will instead of the will of others. That made it easier for me to miss his funeral knowing that it was God's will for me not to go. I was at peace with the decision to stay right where I was. All the while I continued to read and read, and by this time I had finished reading for the second time Gods Word from cover to cover. In this time the Lord shared with me His calling for me, how He wanted me to pray, and what His will was for me. To my amazement I had trouble with my calling at the time and it took me a long time to accept it. By the time you finish reading this you will understand why if you don't already.

Winter time was approaching fast and the Lord had me deal with a situation that weighed very heavy on my heart. The last relationship I was in before I was saved; no doubt my ex-girlfriend who I was willing to spend the rest of my life with. I had a horrific dream and I saw her with someone else besides me. It was in such a way that it caused a pain in my heart I had never felt before. Then the Lord spoke to me after I woke up crying and He said that she was no longer in my life. It was at this point I believe God removed the root of her in my heart by revealing the end of our relationship in this horrific dream. I believe God tore her away, because He knew what stronghold she had over me. And He was not about to compete with anyone or anything in my life. I believe this was another reason why God had me leave Sweetwater in the first place. It was just too many hindrances blocking my relationship with Him. Even though I wanted to know everything about God and wanted nothing more to get closer to Him. I still asked the Lord for a wife and that if He gave me one I would once again go, do, and say whatever it was He wanted me too. God knew my heart and gave me the desire to ask. The Lord said that I would have one and that she would come to me, I believed. At that point I prayed to the Lord to fill her with His Holy Spirit, that she be filled with His wisdom, and understanding so that she may know Him and herself. I also prayed that he would give her discernment and knowledge so that His Will is done in all things. I prayed that God would give me wisdom and discernment concerning all things. I also asked for knowledge and understanding and by faith would receive insight into the things of God.

It was now winter time and my brother had enough of me staying at his place without a job or money. My mom would scrape up change so we could go to the store and buy a big can of oatmeal and bread just so I could eat. Oatmeal and toast, this is what I lived on for a while until I left. And how I left was just as special. My brother and I got into it by me staying at his place and he kicked me out. Since I acted out in my flesh God allowed me to sit outside of his apartment for hours until He decided that it was enough, and that I had learned my lesson. It was a hard knock of many to come until I learned how to deal with my pride, attitude, and emotions.

My brother for the next week or so kept telling me that I was going to have to leave his place. I also felt in my heart that it was time for me to leave as well. I just did not know how the Lord was going to do it. I was watching a speaker on TV and while she was speaking she spoke the words "are you going to get up off of that couch and leave, or are you just going to sit there for the rest of your days and waste away?" It wasn't a day or even a week later that my brother came to me again and said that he would get me a bus ticket to where ever it was that I wanted to go. I just could not stay at his place anymore. Then I knew that this was God and it was time for me to leave. Almost a year later after I was first saved I found myself right back in the same house and town where I gave my life to God, Sweetwater Texas.

This time I knew it would not be for very long. This time I knew the Lord was bringing me to a place to help me go to another level in Him. I was waiting for my cousin to make it back down to Texas from my aunt's house in Indiana. And while waiting I was having conversations with his mom about the word of the Lord that somehow we did not always see eye to eye on. I did not understand it we were all going the same direction in the Lord. Why the difference of opinion of what this or that meant in His Word? Later the Lord revealed to me that not everyone sees Him in the same way. And our relationship with Him and how much He gives Himself to us is going to be based on how much we are willing to let go and give up ourselves for Him. Everyone is not willing to admit there faults, even before the One who already knows that you have them.

It wasn't long before my cousin found his way back to Sweetwater and shortly after spending some time with the family, we were heading to Tulsa Oklahoma where he was attending Oral Roberts University. I had passed through Tulsa plenty of times on vacation with the family, but I had never seen all it had to offer. It had lots of trees and big rolling hills, to me the place was beautiful, the attitudes of the people not so much. But then again you will find the good and the bad in people everywhere you go. Still it would be the place I would call home with my cousin and brother in the Lord for the next year or so.

By the time I was saved my cousin had been saved about five years I believe. Anyway we all got an apartment together and the Lord through my cousin started teaching me about me. I quickly found out that the grace that covered me and my past when I first got saved was lifting. Now I had to start dealing with all of that sin that had me living a lie since birth. See in the beginning God was teaching me about Him and His Son and the way of His Holy Spirit. Now the Lord started showing me how much I was not like Him. And how I needed to get to the place where I could be more like him. This I did not like very well at all, because God began to reveal to me just how bad my issues really were.

First off I got a job at the local Wal-Mart down the street from our apartment, which was cool, because it was walking distance. Second it was one of many tools that God used to show me about me, and what I needed to do to change. God taught me through people I met, through songs I heard on the radio, and through shows I watched on TV. But most of all God taught me about me through the people He had in my life at the time. For about the next year the Lord would show my worst problems and have me deal with it, like sex addiction. He would also have me deal with authority and pride issues. It was at this point in time that I started living everything that I read about in God's Word. And it was like I had every issue that was written in the Word of God. It was now that God was showing me how to deal with them, if I was willing to admit I had the issues in the first place. My cousin taught me a lot in this area, because no matter how much you think you got it together or how important you think you are, in the end you're not. In fact without Jesus our Lord and Savior we would have never existed in the first place. And without balance in everything that we do we would fall and fail God. It is not about how much we can do, it is about how much God can do. And in all things it is Christ who strengthens us to do them all. In other words I needed to stop looking at others when it came to my own issues. Everything that I was going through was because of the decisions that I made, even if it was because I did not have a positive role model growing up. The Lord God was now my positive role model He would now become my Father.

God was not through with me yet, in fact He had not even scratched the surface of bringing me into what He was calling me to be. At this point and time I had no idea of what it really was He was calling me too. Or even what I was going to have to go through to get there.

It had been a year now since my granddad had passed away. While we were just chilling in the living room of our apartment, my brother in the Lord got a message from back where he was from in New York. That one of the twin towers there had been hit by a plane. We were all thinking that it was one of those small planes, until we turned on the news and found out that there was nothing small about what was going on at the World Trade Center. One tower had just been hit by a jumbo jet. And we watched in real time as another one hit the other tower. We thought there is no way that just happened and then they started falling down. Everyone is going to have different thoughts going through their heads, but I was asking God what was this all about? What was He saying to us as a people, and after the initial shock, what next? I never believed that something just happens even before I was saved. I know that everything that happens is for a reason one that we may never understand, especially with a lack of a relationship with God. But I knew in my spirit that there was more to this than just these buildings getting hit by planes and people losing their lives instantly. This was not just a message from terrorist, this was a message from the Great I am, and a strong beginning of many.

Three months later I find myself embarking on another trip back to my home state of Texas. This time God is having me go live with my granny. It seems I have more issues that are in need of some attention. Especially those that have been buried in my mind that I would have rather forgot for good. But I learn the best by hands on example. And God is not in the business of not finishing what He started, so on to the next phase of rebuilding me.

One day searching for a job my aunt had a lead on positions opening up at the local prison. And since I was in the market for a job, I went all in. She helped me fill out the application at her house. But while doing so one of the questions was have you ever committed a crime, or misdemeanor, or felony? Instantly this triggered a flashback of memories of what I went through back in Indiana. Uh oh, grace was lifting in another area of my life and the past was creeping up on me once again. I had no choice but to answer the question honestly. I was living for Jesus Christ now and this was the moment of truth. Never run from your issues, instead embrace them, go to war, and defeat your enemy head on with honesty. This is what I did. I let them know about a situation I had been in in my past. They checked into it and sure enough the problem never left, but it was time to deal with the situation like a man. So we found out what I needed to do to make the wrong right, follow their instructions, and handle it.

Per their instructions I was heading back to Lafayette, Indiana to turn myself in on a now almost five year warrant for failure to appear and other charges. This is how good God is. With the help of Him and my grandmother giving me the necessary amount for me to bail out of jail the moment I set foot in county, was truly a blessing from above. I still had to go to jail and process in and out, but that was just how the system worked. But once again, it gave me an opportunity to know exactly where I stood with God and where I stood with my own feelings. There was a guy who tried me while I was in the cell. And of course he would, because there was only about ten to twelve of us in one little cell. Anyway apparently I was in his spot and he wanted me to move, of course my pride was like "oh hell no you find you another spot". It was a challenge for him and I thought it was going to turn ugly until the Lord stepped in; the guard came by and I just let him have his spot back. All I wanted to do was process out. I did not want to be in there no longer than I had to, so I did the right thing and let it go. At the same time the Lord shared with me that he was going to be there, but I on the other hand was not. I did not take that lightly and I was soon on my way before dinner with a note from the judge to return for court to settle this overdue debt. With another lesson about myself and the power of God under my belt I was now back on a bus heading back to Texas.

Sometime or another I had in my heart to get a truck not long after I was saved. And before I came back to Texas to stay with my granny I became interested in getting my granddads truck. So naturally I asked her about it when I started living with her around 2002. Long story short she said no, but instead took me to get my own. My granny may be biased when it comes to me and her other grandkids, even her own kids, but she had a heart for me and it showed. She loved all of us in her own way and this was one way she showed her love for me. I know God had an influence in her heart for me. But I never really understood that until after I came into the relationship I have with Him today. I will always love my granny and hope that she will find her place with God. And that I will find her in her place up in heaven when I get there.

God blessed me with what was on my heart. And it allowed me to go back to Indiana to court in a much faster way than the bus. The Lord saw a need and provided. There is no one like Him. I even got a job with the city as an animal control officer with the favor of God and the help of my aunt and uncle. Once I had my court ordeal out of the way the judge allowed me to transfer her ruling to the great state of Texas. She gave me community service and suspended my other sentences since I had no other problems. And as long as she never saw me again I would have everything dropped. Only God could pull something off like that considering that I blew her off in the first place, and for so many years on top of that for a battery charge. To say the least I was very grateful and it was definitely an, 'I got closer to God moment in my life.' This was also an opportunity to have a little bonding time with my son who I was ready to spend some time with, despite the rocky past with his mom. She agreed to let him come spend some time with me back in Texas, and that I was thankful for as well. It was a long time coming; in fact before I got saved it had been about three years before.

Colorado City Texas is where my granny and granddad lived and it was a very small town. Smaller than Sweetwater to its east, but it was just like home, when we were kids my grandparents would come and pick us up every weekend to stay with them and we had a blast. But in 2002 and 2003 I was on a different mission in this small little town. Since I was only three years in with my relationship with God, I had some weaknesses and issues that needed to be dealt with. Temptation was all around in a place like this, especially for fresh meat, and vultures were circling overhead. It would not be long before I lost focus and fell right off the island of temptation into its treacherous waters. While I was on patrol with my job I caught the eye of a fine little sister who lived in the area. I can't help to remember that I was checking her out as well. And for me to say that you would not know what happened next would be completely ridiculous, especially when we both were attracted to each other.

You will always learn a lesson from one or two ways, the easy way or the hard way. Unfortunately for me I always gravitated to the latter. And when it came to this particular female I found myself in the same old boat, trouble.

After I first got saved, I was told that I would need to ask God to break all soul ties that I had developed in past relationships with women. I completely jumped on that, because I did not want anything getting in the way of knowing the God who delivered me from certain death. Soul ties, the way I understood it, was after you have sex with a person you take on that person's spirit and they take on yours. God said in His Word (and I will paraphrase) that when two people come together as in a sexual way the both of them become one. So it made perfect sense to me that you become who you are with. And if that is not enough for you, how about the thought of sexually transmitted diseases? I have had sex and unprotected sex at that, with a lot of women. And I know what it is like to have such diseases. So I had to deal with this problem of soul ties quickly. I asked God in faith to break from me all of these spirits of other women. Then not only are you dealing with all women you have been with. Now you are dealing with all of the people they have slept with as well. So it is a chaotic chain of events. And it also explains the reason I started having erratic behaviors or started taking on someone else's characteristics after being with them for a while. Even after knowing all of this I chose to enter into a relationship with a complete stranger. And worse yet a person who had a very limited relationship (or better yet a person who did not seem to be having) the same relationship like I was trying to have with God. But this girl kept pressing and my brain and hormones was tricking me in to believe that, 'she could be your wife.' I gave into temptation and a quick friendship turned into multiple sexual encounters. Did I really know what I was doing? Well when it comes to the little head over writing the big head that would be an easy no. I was easily being deceived by Satan and or his demons; either way my decision to sleep with her was a mistake. But in like all mistakes there was learning in the midst of all of the chaos, or this should be the case after you make a mistake. God was showing me that I could not be in denial when it came to my feelings, especially those that are monumental giants. Oh help me, because I had a serious thing with the opposite sex a complete struggle of lust if you will. At this part of my life grace was lifting as well, and it was getting to the point where if any girl or woman looked at me like they liked me I was also looking at them as well. But this was part of my nature. And it was instilled at or even before birth. God was revealing to me that I needed to address this issue. Looking back, and I did not notice it then, but every encounter I had with a woman was about sex and then conversation. And if conversation was involved, it was used to have sex. Was I that bad? You bet I was, but there is a God who loved me through my worst days including the ones after being saved. Because this sister I was seeing at the time came in just as I was settling into my community service from my court case, and she was in hot pursuit to get me. We talked for a while, did what we did, and at the end of the day it turned into one of the biggest drama stories in my life. The point of this is not the drama story, but it is a demonstration of how good God is. Because after all I went through with her I learned I had a weakness for women. And she would not be the only one I would encounter after being saved.

Failing and Falling

This was my down fall, this was my meat and potatoes of destruction, sex everything that had to do with sex, and more sex. Pornography, sex tapes, videos, magazines, stamina pills, you name it if it had sex in it I was in it. Sex was my goliath and it had me by the balls choking me to death. But I had to see that it was killing me before God could do anything about it. The only way for me to see just how gigantic my struggle was killing me was to turn me aloes in it. Leave me in that mess until I got the picture. Leave me in it until I got sick of it having control of my life.

This particular girl was not my wife and God made it a point for me to know that. On the other hand my family life took a drastic turn for the worst as well. After my temporary job as an animal control officer ended for the first time (to catch you up to speed it was temporary, because I took the place of a guy who was in the military). Anyway after it ended I was left looking for another job. Here I was living with my grandmother, no job, a truck note and my son was down from Indiana for the summer. This did not sit well with my dad and probably everyone else around him. They believe that you should work in order to eat and I absolutely agree with that philosophy. What I did not agree with was the lack of communication in delivering a civilized message that would bring a person up without tearing him to pieces when he is already down. Like for instance when things really went downhill with my dad and I after I told him that God was calling me to be a minister. I could see the look of whatever all in his face after I told him one night on my granny's front porch. He was the second family member and one of the first people I told period since God revealed this revelation to my own spirit. Well it was not long after that I felt in my spirit that it was time to leave Colorado City, and that something was about to happen. In the year or so I was here God dealt with a very heavy issue in my life. And it was one that kept me from having the kind of relationship He wanted to have with me. That issue was how I viewed women in relation to sex and how I treated my own body in relation to sex. In other words controlling masturbation, pornography, and sex with women instead of those things controlling me would have to be learned if I was going to grow in God. This was a new level in God. It was a lessoned learned and now it was time to move on. How did I know you may ask? Let's just say the Lord will make it very plain and clear. On July 4th, I believe it was in 2003 my dad and some of my aunt and uncles came over to the house. I don't remember the details in what triggered this dispute, but all hell broke out (again) with my dad and I. It was not good and I knew this day was coming for a long time. The tension lingered in the air between my dad and me for a long time especially after I told him I was becoming a minister. This was God's way of telling me that it was time to go and that He was closing a door on another chapter. They pretty much kicked me and my son Quindon out of my grandmother's house that day. My aunt even wanted to call the cops on me all because I had something to say, and they did not want to hear what I had to say. Despite my short comings and failures God was still using me to do His will. He was also training me at the same time to honor my initial vow to Him at my born again birth. So I packed up what I had at the time put it in the truck and me and my son left. We were on the road heading back to where I previously came from just a little over a year before, Tulsa Oklahoma. We stayed in Tulsa for a little while and then I took my son back home to Indiana. After that I came back to Tulsa to stay with my brothers in the Lord to get ministered to and receive wise counsel even if I didn't want to hear it. That's one thing about God, if you're really trying to have a relationship with Him He is not going to tell you what you want to hear. He is going to tell you what you need to hear and it is not always pretty. Sometimes it can be downright brutal to hear, but in order to grow in God it is very necessary. I stayed for a few months or so in Oklahoma and then my granny got in touch with me to see how I was doing. We talked for a while about what happened and she said that she never wanted me to leave. In the end she wanted me to come back, deep down inside she knew what happened with my dad and the way it happened was wrong. So by the time the New Year came I was back in Texas again. And on top of that I got my old job back after the military guy left for duty again. Working with the police department as an animal control officer was a good experience for me. I also met some pretty cool people. One in particular will always be remembered in my life, and she was one of the dispatchers for the city. She was a lot of fun to be around and we talked about almost everything. I met her son and her niece and they became like family to me. One day while I was shooting the breeze with her at work another niece of hers came in and gave me a look I will never forget. Put it this way if I were a target I would have been painted red and there was no way they could have missed me. We became real close friends real fast and if you thought I learned my lesson from the last relationship, not yet, I was still living in the drama I was creating. What was it going to take for me to get the picture? The relationship went on for a short while until the Lord saw fit for me to end it. It was funny how God used the previous relationship I was in to end the current relationship. I had no attention to hurt any one of the women I had relationships with. I just made bad decisions that cost me and them dearly. I was just a sucker for women and would go out of my way to get what I wanted. I mean I drove four hours one time just to see a girl who already was in a relationship with someone and had two kids by this guy. Hey she kept telling me that she was ending the relationship with him and at first I believed it. But in the end I was BAMBOOZLED.

In the middle of all of this madness God was still blessing me through all of my mistakes and bad choices. When I was about nine or ten my mother use to play records from time to time on her stereo and it was the most beautiful sound I had ever heard as a kid. So I was always fascinated about how music was made. I would listen to it for hours rocking back and forth in a chair off to myself just listening. One day my grandmother bought me a boom box with a cassette player that had those LED lights. The lights would bounce back and forth and it had big speakers on each side. Anyway at the time this thing was my favorite thing in the whole world. And hip hop had not long made it big in west Texas, sometime in the early eighty's. Well I got a hold of some of the hottest music I had ever heard, like Beat Street and Breaking and it was over for me. I wanted to know everything about this music. How they made it, what they used to make it, and what was their inspiration in making it, because I was hooked. One day I was listening to some music outside and my cousin stopped to check me out for a minute. He said he had a new tape called the Egyptian Lover. So he went and got it and the next thing you know we had a block party right on Hughes Street in the center of the projects. Seeing all of the kids dancing and moving in the street to sounds coming from my box made me want to pee my pants, and I knew I wanted to do something with music sometime in my life. Over time life deterred me from following my initial dream, but I did manage to complete a course in Audio Recording as an engineer in 1996 and picked up making beats in the late eighty's. It was just something being able to work with people in an art that was about self-expression. So fast forward to two thousand and four, and once again a passion that was lost for seven years had been rekindled by the meeting of a young cat just about to graduate high school. He was a rapper and he wasn't that bad, but one thing he had was passion, determination, and most of all a mouth piece. I always told him he could talk a golf ball through a water hose. But it was something about him that made me want to restart a mission I could not complete before I was saved due to life issues. So I asked my grandmother if she would help me get a keyboard. When she did we went to work on making some music. I made about five or six beats on this thing that were keepers. After he wrote his raps to them we took them to his cousin's studio to record and put them on CD.

One thing about this dude and his whole family, they had talent. We had a full production. He even involved his sister who sang, well, I was impressed and my entrepreneur wheels started turning with ideas. I decided to go all out and use every resource I knew about to help get this kid a record deal, including taking a loan out on my truck to pay for a recording studio of my own. I prayed and asked the Lord for a small recording studio and to my amazement He allowed it and I got the loan. Anyway the young lady I was seeing at the time helped me take photos of us for the demo. She also believed in us enough to help with the submission cost. Something that she did not have to do and no matter what I would be forever grateful, because I knew how excited this guy was about his talent and getting a recording contract. After we sent the demo off to a talent agency I went to work purchasing new gear for the recording studio. I mean I had drum machines, keyboards and even worked in studios before, but I never had my own full digital studio. This was like a dream come true and I was excited as a virgin on her wedding night after everything came in. But with all things God gives you, I had no idea what I was going to go through after opening up the studio. More like what I put myself through with my eager ambition to have an artist make it big from a small town like Colorado City. I don't think anyone else saw the same vision I saw. And if they did they did not realize how much work it would be. At the end of the day I believe I let my business side override any real fun in having a studio in the first place. Oh well, we did have some fun recording songs and yes there was a record deal involved with an independent record label. But this label wanted us to invest too much of our own time and money marketing our own stuff. I wouldn't say that it was completely bogus, but it was too much for us to take on right then. Without going into too much detail I just chalked it up as it not being God's will to land a deal at that time. It was so close and yet so far away. And as the recording dream faded away, so did the relationship with the girl I was with come to an end.

I continued to record in the studio until my job with the city played out for the last time. And in between that time one of the guys I was recording with had a female cousin he wanted me to meet.

Side note; when it comes to a counterfeit say like money, it looks real it may even smell real but there is something about it that is just not right. It did not come from the right source, in other words the wrong person sent it. My case and point of every woman I have ever been with sexually, or not after establishing my relationship with the Lord. And before I lose you let me get into this last relationship to tie it all together.

After the animal control job I landed a job at a state hospital so I started driving about forty miles each way a day. Anyway my man described his cousin to me and I was like yeah sounds good. Well I knew in my mind that God said that my wife would come to me, but I also struggled with when. So I wanted to know more about her, because she could be "the one". She could be the one God said would be for me, I played that over and over in my head until it stuck. It stuck so well that when I finally met her in person everything in me was like "she is the one." You better believe my mind was made up and everything that followed was based on that decision to believe she was. I mean we hit it off so fast that she just had to be, but was it a fatal attraction? We talked and we talked some more, she had a daughter I met her, she had a family I met them, she had friends I began to meet them. In fact things moved so quickly that within a month and due to the location of my new job I was moving in with her. She lived in the same town as my job and we wanted to take the relationship to the next level. After all I believed she was "the one." And I had peace about the whole thing. Or was that my hormones? Even before I moved in with her my excitement lead into a sexual encounter and it was after I moved in, the drama began. Do not get me wrong I would never try to bash anyone, but for continuity I must tell what I experienced on my journey with God. Before I moved in I started having these funny sensations in my private area. I didn't think anything of it until a few days later then it started burning-it felt like I had razor blades coming out of my penis when I went to the bathroom. In my past I have had a sexual transmitted disease before so I knew that it had to be no doubt just that. I made it a point for both of us to go to a clinic and get checked out, because this was a serious thing. The clinic tested us and sure enough we had gonorrhea, I was hot, but all I could think about right then was moving on and getting better. That was actually the second sign of I was not where I was supposed to be, but God allowed it anyway. The first sign was that she told me she did not have any hot water at her house which I did not mind. The reason that she didn't have any hot water was troubling for me though, especially after I found the reason to be a lie. The first sign I was not supposed to be there was the fact we started on a lie. I looked out the window of the kitchen one day while washing dishes and saw that there was not a gas meter in the back yard. I am no meter reader, but from working with the city I knew that it takes a meter to have gas, no meter no gas. So I asked her about it and she said that she did not want me to think that she could not pay her bills or maintain a home. You know I consider myself a somewhat compassionate person. All I wanted was a solid foundation of a relationship. We all have problems and I could care less about no gas we can get gas, what we could not have was an honest relationship from the start. Charge it to the game move on and let's see what else happens. Ok, I thought the STD and now the gas was just minor glitches, all relationships go through stuff. But from what I did learn from my relationship with the Lord you forgive and move on. We had quite a few things in common, but the more we got to know each other one thing we definitely had in common was that we were both still married, which by the way was the explanation of her having an STD. Contracted from a cheating husband not even knowing she carried it for so long. Little ghost in the closet started trickling out like that over time, and yet I was still convinced she was the one for me. Mainly due to the fact that when we first started talking my number one question for her was "are you saved, do you believe in Jesus Christ?" Her answer was yes and I knew that she had to be the one. I had peace so I thought. Until the peace I once held started ending and our arguments started beginning. I thought what in the hell is going on? Surely if she was my wife we would not be having all of this trouble. If God put us together it would be His responsibility to keep us together no matter what we went through. But if it was not His will for us to be together, the relationship was going to end in time. And in a short amount of time we went through a lot and many of secrets were uncovered.

But I still stuck by her side believing she was for me. On top of that she stood by me with all of my secrets I was beginning to be confused. The Lord started revealing little by little true motives of the whole relationship with us and hers with God. You cannot fool God. And if your motives are not pure or good God will reveal the real you, and there is no hiding from The Almighty. Then God had enough and revealed the truth about the whole thing. He sent my cousin with a clear and to the point message "she is not your wife." At that point I had to make a decision and it was a clear one. I had to leave repenting was not an option it had to be done. So be it. No matter how good things looked on the outside things on the inside was counterfeit. I swallowed my pride packed my things and moved back in with my grandmother.

The Real Deal

Now God has a habit of showing you good in the midst of chaos. One night after work some friends and co-workers came over to the house to mess around in the studio before I left town. One of them just happened to be a female and her name was Jennifer. We were just friends, but little did I know that God had something else in store. One day Jennifer and I were walking a patient together at our job. He didn't talk very well, but he would just keep on saying "pronounce, pronounce" as we walked him up and down the hall. We had no idea what he was talking about until he made Jennifer and I hold hands while he said "pronounce." After that it became clear to me just what he was trying to say and probably more than that, what God was revealing.

It wasn't long after I moved back to Colorado City that I was down on my knees praying asking God for forgiveness and clarity of His Will concerning what had been revealed. I did not want to make another mistake in my decisions of taking on another relationship. My mind deceived me once it could do it again. Rushing into things I was used to and it was also getting old causing many problems in the long run. This time I had to make sure what was in my spirit was coming from The Spirit and not from my emotions. So I was prostrate blocking out all distractions asking the Lord if it was His Will for Jennifer to become my wife. Everything in me came back a simple and gentle yes. It did not take long after that to start talking more just as friends, but God moved things along quickly after revealing His Will. I had become a supervisor at our job so now that Jennifer and I were talking more, questions began to rise about the involvement of our relationship. It didn't look good on my job and I knew that something had to give if this was something the Lord was ordaining in the first place. It wasn't long after that that the very thing I struggled with before would be the very thing God would us to allow me to leave, my temper. I was a pretty good employee, did the best I could at my job, and it did not go unnoticed. So when the hospital needed new supervisors I was one of the people they chose. I was really nervous and I really did not want the position considering I had only been there for about six months. I knew it had to be the Will of God, because other than asking God for healing of my body and a wife I never would have asked for a supervisor position. Anyway one day while on duty stress of the job and other factors of life caused me to lose my temper. In return I tried to stop a patient from leaving his room pushing him down making him hit his head as a result. One of my workers saw me reported it and in the end I resigned. I knew I was in the wrong, the damage was done and it did not need to go any further. God made an example out of me that day showing me that, one I still had an issue with anger. Two He was ending my stay in that place and three He was closing the door. Jennifer and I continued to talk and build a relationship. When we went to her dad and stepmom with the news of our relationship we encountered resistance. First of all I was black and she was Hispanic that was the first response, you should stick to your own kind. But I was not looking at her as any particular race I was looking at her as she was the one God was choosing for me, she just happened to be Hispanic. This is the misconception of people in their lack of a relationship with The Most High God. He doesn't see color in people, He just sees people and it is the very reason why we limit God and ourselves. We focus more on what brings us down instead of what builds us up and where is the peace in that? In all, I dealt with resistance in my own family so even though it was disappointing not being accepted at first, I kept moving forward. Forward in Gods will and forward in the relationship He was giving me with Jennifer. After I was gone from the state hospital for a little while the Lord came to me again and told me that it was time to go and take your wife with you. This was interesting because I had asked her to marry me sometime before and she also knew that legally I was still married to my first wife ten years prior. And yet God was saying take her and go, so we packed up what we had and moved back to Tulsa Oklahoma with our "brothers". Let me back up just a minute before you think I took a club to this woman's head and made her go with me to Oklahoma. I asked her to pray and ask God if this was His Will for her to do what he was telling me without telling her what He told me. One of the reasons for me making sure haste was not making waste. This was a big decision and I was really tired of ruining other people's lives due to my choices. So if she believed in her heart God was leading her then we would both go. If not, then only I would. And that is how we started our journey together. Every decision was based on what God was telling us and not what we were telling each other.

Back in Tulsa in 2005 we quickly went to work on finding a job. We found one at a major appliance factory. I continued to learn more about myself through everyday activity with friends, co-workers, and everyone God had put around me at the time. I found out very quickly that the issues I had were great and grace was being lifted off of them. (What issues?) Self-esteem, pride, jealousy, envy, selfishness, and anger were just a few issues with power over me. I knew I had to deal with them head on. As God showed them to me, I had to stand and fight them instead of run away like I did before the Lord gave me the strength to deal with them. So once He allowed a situation to arise that showed off an issue I had. I just admitted it to myself and the Lord that I had that problem, turned it over to Him and then let it go? If I had been in denial of an issue, which at times I was, then the problem would continue to follow me and grow in strength at the same time. But for so long I had been bound up in chains with the same issues and all I wanted was to be free. I had to do whatever it took to get free of everything that Satan had power over me. And now God had giving me a family. If I could not be free how was I supposed to show them how to be free? Speaking of being free, the marriage I entered into while still in the Marine Corps was now officially over. I received divorce papers in the mail the same year Jennifer and I moved up to Oklahoma. How is that for a conformation and freedom in one shot? God is a good God all the time.

Jennifer and I worked at the appliance factory for almost five or six months and even started a mail order business. Then one day while we were washing clothes at a laundry mat I saw an ad in the paper about going to school for radio broadcasting. Since I had already been to audio engineering school and a music buff, I decided to look into it. After I prayed about it and checked out the school I believed it was God's Will for me to go. Just to make sure, if they accepted me I was going to go, but if they didn't then I would know it was not His Will. I applied they accepted and soon after I became a full time student at a radio broadcasting school. That meant Jennifer and I would both be giving up our jobs at the factory, because we only had one vehicle. With it being so far out it would not agree with my new schedule. And it also meant that the income would change in the house we shared with our brothers. This brought on a new challenge and a new struggle that we failed to communicate with everyone in the house. The fact that we did not talk about what was going on with us forced us into an uncertain situation, and had our brother a little upset since they would have to take up the slake in bills. One thing I did learn from that situation is that even if you believe that God is directing you in a certain direction, when there are multiple people involved you need to talk about it with them. It is just a common courtesy and it develops/maintains positive relationships with family. You will cut down all guessing and confusion without seeming nosey, if it just gets talked about in the beginning before a decision is going to be made that involves everyone.

In February 2006 I started my schooling in radio broadcasting and around the same time Jennifer and I found out that God had blessed us with our first child together. Back at home God had appointed my cousin who indeed was my brother in the Lord over me to instruct and minister to me His Will. I knew my brother played a significant role in the development of my character, but because I always saw him as my little cousin it was hard for me to accept it. And what made it even worse was the fact that when I first moved to Tulsa with him. God spoke through him about how I chose to deal with the biggest issue I had, which was sex. I resented my cousin even though I knew it was God speaking through him, because only God could know how I was trying to deal with that issue. I knew this because my cousin was not even their or even inside of my head. And he spoke about what I was doing, that was a wakeup call for me. But it would also stir up another issue of pride, resentment and envy that would affect my relationship with my cousin and the Lord for a long time. So when my brother would come to me with a word from the Lord, God knows there were many times I took the message with a grain of salt. This hindered my growth in a big way and caused my relationship with God and my brother to suffer, because I refused to see him the way the Lord saw him. God placed him in my life as a teacher and deliverer of His Word and because I only would view him as my cousin I limited God. In all of my arrogance the Lord blessed me anyway. I did not go unpunished though, at times my sons mom from Indiana would call and cuss me out or say negative things like I wasn't a man, because I didn't have the money to send my son. It was another learning experience that showed just how much I was or was not growing in the Lord. At first I failed every stress test that God sent my way due to my own ways. It was not until I started letting go of all of my pride that I slowly started passing His tests.

During the summer while I was still in school the Lord showed me favor and allowed my son to come down during his school break. It would also serve as test of my character and whether or not I still was suffering from anger and temper issues. His mom would let him come down for the summer. And yet while he was here in Tulsa when it was time for him to leave if I could not give her specifics of when I could get him back, she would start drama. I on the other hand believed God would make a way for him to get back home to Indiana. And indeed He did, because I don't know if she was scared that I was going to try to keep him or what? But she came and got him herself and that is how God worked that out. It was a test of my character and whether or not I would walk away from confrontation. God was showing me about me and how much work that had to be done in me to become more like His Son who came before me. I could not let my emotions dictate my surroundings. They could not have more power over me than God. It would not be beneficial to my growth. About four months later radio school was coming to a close and I learned a lot about myself and others. One thing that stuck out the most was the fact that my instructor once said, "you have to be careful of who you step on when you're on your way to the top. Because the same people you see going up will be the same people you see coming down. And if they helped you going up, they probably will not as you come down." I heard this saying before, but the reason it stuck out so much this time was because I knew God was calling me for something big and this word had an anointing. This time I had a different perspective on it after I heard it. I also learned that there were different learning styles academically and that I was not as dumb as I thought. Back in high school I just barely graduated and I thought it was because I wasn't smart enough to pass the grade. Turns out I just had a different learning style from other kids and also my learning suffered being easily distracted. When I went to audio engineering school I graduated with honors and now once again I was graduating from radio school with honors. This was proof that I was not as dumb as I thought; I just had to focus and know that I had an on hands learning style. Once I learned that, it became less of a challenge to succeed in an academic environment.

After I graduated from American Broadcasting School in December 2006 and Jennifer getting closer to delivery, we made a trip back down to Texas for the holidays. I could sense that we were going to be down there for a little while, but once we were back it became apparent we was moving back. I believe it had a lot to do with my attitude at the time. It was a little on the negative side and I was always on edge with my brothers, in hind sight the situation I was in and the situation God was about to put us in was to get all of that negative stuff out of me. The thought of my grandmother letting us come back to live with her was not in her plans and yet it was in Gods. So she reluctantly let us come back to stay and I imaging it didn't sit well with the rest of the family either. Did we catch hell, oh yes we did? In fact we did not have a warm welcome at all from some of my family and whether they would admit it or not, jealousy played a vital role.

Jennifer stayed in Texas while I went back with my brothers to Tulsa to get our stuff. Just before I left, the Lord spoke through my brother as we talked about us leaving and He said "the woman you are with is your wife." This was a conformation despite whatever everybody else thought or believed. If The Most High God said she was my wife then no matter my past or situation, that is who she was. We caught a lot of crap over the fact that we did not have official papers saying that we were legally married while staying with my grandmother. It wasn't right. Especially from a bible point of view, but then I also questioned where they read that and if they did, how they interpreted that scripture on their own. I believe religion will kill you faster than any disease. If I rely on religion instead of faith walking around dead is a reality. A real relationship with Jesus is what I longed for, and I believe it is the only thing that will allow you to live without fear. It is fear that causes us to lie to one another, to fight one another, and to be jealous of one another. Fear causes envy and hate to take root in our hearts, and it is a giant silent killer of our very existence. The more we feed our fear the fatter the devil gets, and I needed to learn how to trust God more in order for me to stop feeding Satan. And yet, I was eating at a table in the presence of my enemy's.

On February 7th my granny came into this world to begin her legacy that would eventually spawn me. Three generations later on the same day my own daughter was born to begin hers. It was an event that only God could be in control of and one that no doubt revealed my family's secrets as well as my own. It's one thing to have secrets, but it's another thing to have secrets and pretend that you don't, and confess that you have a relationship with Jesus. He will expose them in time one way or another. How can I teach anything to anyone if I fail to deal with my own problems while finding fault with everyone else around me? This was a strategic placement by God for me, my wife, and new daughter Gabrielle. I caught negative vibes from my side of the family on my dad's side and also on my wife's side of the family on her dad's side. And because of the fear of God no one had the nuts to step up and say how they really felt. It was always a behind the back moment, but it was obvious how they felt by their actions of how they treated us, or didn't treat us. One day I overheard my granny say while she was talking to one of my aunts, "I wish they would pack up there stuff and leave." I even asked her one day in a conversation we were having that if she did not want us in her house anymore that all she had to do was say so and we would leave. It was always, 'no you don't have any other place to go' or 'where are you going to go?' The truth is that it was God's Will for us to be right where we were at. And to suffer from the very ones who were closer to us. A growing period, one that would drive me over the edge and force me to want to give up life itself, but I was a coward when it came to committing suicide. So I let God know that I hated the whole situation. At times my anger even caused me to argue back with my grandmother. I was being tested, pulled, pruned, and purged of everything God was trying to get rid of inside of me. And He was using my own family to do it.

At the same time He was revealing dark secrets I never knew existed from me and them. One thing was for sure I knew that I did not want to stay where I was. And the only way to move on was to deal with every issue the Lord was exposing in me. We were in Texas for a year. And in that time I had three jobs. Not because I was lazy, but it was the favor of God blessing one better job after another. The last one I gave up, because my wife could not stand staying at home and would rather go out on her own to work. So we swapped duties, she found a job and I stayed home with the baby. No doubt God's will and I quickly found out why my wife would rather work. God was cleaning out all of our skeletons in the closet and fear of man was not an option. Staying where we were at was forcing us to deal with weak areas in our lives that were hindering our relationship with God. We were all getting on each other's nerves stepping on each other's toes invading each other's spaces in order to deal with some of our biggest issues, us. One time Gabby fell off of the bed when she was just starting to move around and she cried like I had never heard her cry before. I picked her up to make sure she was alright and held her in my arms to comfort her. My granny was very fond of this little girl being that she was her great grandchild born on her birthday. Anyway she came in yelling at me asking me what was wrong with her, what did I do to her, why was she crying like that? Each time I told her I got her now she fell off of the bed while I stepped away real quick to get her lotion. She just kept on saying Gabby didn't just fall off of the bed that I did something to her. I had no reason to lie as God is my witness, but my emotions kicked in and it lead me to get upset and blow up at my granny for not excepting my word. After I calmed down I apologized to my granny for my outburst like I did other times I put my emotions before the Lord. This was a test of my faith, and trust in God, and I didn't always past the test. There was one event that took me by surprise and yet it was not a surprise at all. That was the day my aunt blew up at me for speaking up about how they really felt about us staying at grannies. It is not right to bash people so I will just say that I was seeking the truth about the matter and had the nuts to ask about it. The crap hit the fan and my aunt was not very happy about being confronted. The fact that she got that upset was enough for me to know her true feelings about the matter. I thank God for growing me up, because I could have easily went to her level and she was already in my face like she wanted to fight me for bringing such a thing up. All I wanted to know is why we were treated like we didn't exist and everyone else was treated civilized? I learned a lot about myself, others, and God in that you can't hide the truth. And that God has your back in ways we will never understand no matter the situation.

It was not all bad in the year we spent in Colorado City growing ourselves up. I did meet a musician by the name of Coley who brought the kid out of me again when it came to studio recording. Coley had come over to my grandmother's house to fix her stove. We got to talking and I found out that he had just finished self-recording his CD. I also found out he had no idea how he was going to mix it. That was funny to me because, I told him that I went to an audio engineering school and would be glad to check over his work. Long story short I helped him mix his entire project, we learned a lot from each other and remain friends to this day. God has a way of putting people in your life that causes you to grow in one way or another, who has what you need when you need it. Coley was not a very spiritual person, but he and I both realized it was not a coincidence that we both met. What I liked the most about Coley was that he is a laid back kind of guy and he had soul. I just hope I planted a seed that will bear fruit one day, because he is such a cool friend to have around.

Anyway around the same time we arrived in Texas was about the same time we ended up leaving. It had been a year facing many demons, and then God allowed us to leave and face many more. Talking to my brother on the phone I asked him if we could come back to Tulsa. And because of my infancy in the past of causing confusion he agreed, only if we could keep peace in the house between us all. After going through what we had in the past year with living in chaos, I had grown past chaos and confusion and was ready to move on. I told him indeed that there was nothing more important to me than living in peace and that without peace I have nothing. We seemed to be on the same page with keeping peace between us as our main objective and in January of 2008 we moved back to Tulsa Oklahoma. God has a way of showing you your wrongs and addressing them, disciplining you, and even puts you in a situation that should allow you to change. It is then entirely up to you how long you will stay in that situation before you decided to change. As for me, ever since I came into a relationship with the Lord I made a vow to do His will and I never wanted to stay in a situation that would hold me back from that.

After we moved back to Tulsa it was the will of the Lord for my wife to go to work outside of the house and for me to stay home with our daughter. This would be another test of my faith, because I would rather be out making a decent living instead of being cooped up like a caged pigeon. But I continued to trust in the Lord and despite what any of my family or my wife's family thought about how or why I did what I was doing, I stood my ground believing in God. So Jennifer got a job at the same place my cousin was working at and worked it by the grace of God. Meanwhile the Lord continued to test me in my ways exposing more of my attitude, temper, and just fine tuning my very being. The Lord was constantly preparing me for His work and for His will. I was not always a willing vessel and at times became rebellious to doing it Gods way. Sometimes I would not listen to what God had to say about my ways. And it even got to a point where I would say that I did not even want to praise the Lord anymore, because I felt like I was in too much pain. Pain caused by my own actions, and pain caused by what the Lord was putting me through. Over time I quickly lost focus of what the Lord was trying to do in me and started focusing on the pain, forgetting what I had said in the beginning of our relationship. In which the Lord reminded me of that after He said I should be ashamed of myself for saying that I did not even want to praise Him, because of what I was going through. So I remembered what I vowed to the Lord and repented asking God to forgive my selfishness. After being reminded of just how Jesus died on the cross for sinners like me. I quickly sucked up my little pain and told God that no matter what He took me through again, I would never again say I would not praise Him. I had so many issues dealing with myself that at times

I was a burden to my wife and everybody in the house where we stayed. God was purging me of my past and He knew just how to do it. He also chose the right woman for me, because for one calling myself a saved Christian I was acting far from it. And I knew that it was God who had put us together and he was keeping us together. Looking back on how I treated the very people in my own house I was a complete asshole at times. And my wife had to put up with my crap when she did not deserve to be talked to the way I did, or even worse not talking at all. This was the very reason the Lord had me stay home and Jennifer go out and work. I was forced to deal with my demons and at the same time while Jen was out doing her thing she was dealing with hers. God is a good God and He knows just how to get you to a point where you can deal with yourself, all I had to do was allow Him too, and He changed me. Changing me still, I continued to learn more about myself. After one test was past another test showed up and I started on another level all over again. In the midst of dealing with all of my issues of life, the Lord was blessing us again. And we found out that we were going to have another baby. If this did not add insult to injury God said in His Word to be fruitful and multiply. He also said that He would supply all of our needs, but what He didn't say was how. The fact that I started out my relationship with the Lord by faith, I had no choice but to continue to live by the same faith in Jesus who delivered me from death the first time.

Jennifer worked at her job up until the time she gave birth to our second child, a son, and we named him Immanuel. In every act of Gods goodness the devil tries to counteract with the showing of his evil hand. After our first child Gabrielle was born she had trouble breathing on her own and Immanuel also had a problem. He had jaundice and had to be put under ultraviolent light in order to get better. But in all of this it was Gods will for us to go through this test. After all, were we going to focus on the problem or were we going to focus on God who was in control of the problem. So I believed in what God could do and not what was in plain sight, after all a test is only good if you can pass it. Immanuel got over his jaundice and was off of his ultraviolent treatment a lot sooner than what anybody expected. We were back completely relying on God for our provisions. Jen never returned to her job after Immanuel was born and we believe we were doing what the Lord was leading us to do. This part of our struggle was indeed a challenge. Not only was I not working, but my wife was not either. Now instead of three people out of four working in the house it was only two. God was testing us all and we were all being stretched to the last. The challenges we faced just kept on growing and as time went on, so did we. It was not long before Manny was crawling, sitting up, and trying to walk. Then the Lord would pass on another blessing and give us another child. Jennifer was pregnant again with our third child and it would no doubt be the biggest test of our faith yet. Throughout this entire pregnancy the Lord did not allow us to go through any prenatal care, and it was quite daunting. At this point we had to trust in God like we had never done before. With Gabby and Manny, there was a doctor involved with the whole pregnancy, including the place where we would go for delivery? But this one was very different in that the entire nine months went by with only the word of the Lord to guide us in what we should do. In the meantime to add to the challenge God lifted grace on another area of my life that had some concern of mine for a long time.

Before the Lord brought Jennifer into my life I kept receiving information that I had another child in Indiana besides my son Quindon. Anyway one year after he came down to visit my cousin and I drove him back home. And while we were there we decided to stop by the place this old relationship happened just to see the little girl who was supposedly mine. She was a beautiful little girl maybe about three or four at the time. She was really smart for her age already knowing how to operate a computer and showing us what she could do on it. It was pretty impressive, but we were there to see if she looked anything like me. Maybe we were just in denial and that is one of the reasons my cousin went with me to be a second pair of unbiased eyes for me, but neither one of us could see me in her. Little did we know fast forwarding some six or seven years later, the paternity test would catch up to me again. This time I had to face the music and take care of this once and for all. I would not pretend to deny the existence of this test any longer. And to prove whether or not this now much older little girl was my daughter or not, I had to get a DNA test done. If she was mine even though I had only what God was giving me at the time, which was Him, I would be her dad and take care of my responsibilities the best way that I could. So I took the test and it came back a month or two later; she was daughter. My life became more complicated in that one moment than any other. And getting closer to the Lord was my only option. It would seem that complication also brought a sense of completion as well. No more wondering if Kiara (pronounced like the lion in the movie) was my daughter, now indeed she was. And now I waited on the Lord to put me in a position to spend some time with her and to get to know now my oldest little girl.

Living by Faith

About three months later the moment of truth came with Jennifer and I and our third child. Considering that we didn't have any prenatal care was not even scratching the surface of our concerns. What hospital would we go to, what would they say about us not having a doctor? And most important what would our baby be like coming out of the womb without a doctor only trusting entirely in God? When it came down to it we had no time to think about any of those things. Jennifer handled pain really well and when it was time, it was time. The reality set in with my cousin as well being that he had to drive us to the hospital, and he did so as fast as he could. Straight to the closest hospital we went. This is the part where it got real interesting real fast, because the first thing they asked us when we got there was who is your doctor? Who is your doctor? With Jennifer and I looking at each other real quick as she lie there in pain having contractions we gently said, "we do not have one." They immediately had this look on their face like uh oh here we go prepare for the worst. Indeed as they checked her she was clearly about to have this baby and they had no time to wonder the outcome, she was already dilated a nine. They asked a few questions and then talked their doctor language about preparing for the baby to be breach or something else they have seen with people who use drugs. Clearly I could see where this was going.

Now this whole time during the pregnancy Jen and I had a name picked out for the baby, even though we were not sure what we were having. Believing real strongly for a boy we picked out a boy's name, Jeremiah after the great prophet. However at the end of the day after all the push and shove, the little boy we believed we were having turned out to be a girl. We were not prepared for any girl names at all, because in our hearts we wanted a boy. So on the spot after we saw here and looked how healthy and beautiful she was we named her Miah. And because she was brought about by faith, trusting entirely in God for her deliverance, we gave her the full name of Miah Faith Bender. God showed us that day that He was in control and by faith nothing is impossible for Him. The staff at the hospital had to do their normal routine and try to make sense of why we did not have any medical care with this pregnancy. So the social worker would not let us have Miah in the room until the drug test they were running came back negative. Meanwhile she drilled my wife in that this or that could have happened or she could have had serious medical problems or worse death. And in all of this even though we were in a faith based hospital she was looking at this whole situation in a worldly point of view. We on the other hand took God for His Word. We did as He instructed. At the end of the day and after they ran their test she came out healthier than her sister and her brother. No medical conditions until after she was a year old. She developed Eczema which had nothing to do with prenatal care. The social worker and the hospital was not going to let Miah go home with us until they could get the test results back, but Miah had to be able to soil her diaper before they could even start the test. We waited and waited and they were about to send us home without her until she finally went, she had all negative test. Glory is to God Almighty creator of heaven and earth and our very existence. We were all going home from the hospital together. And no matter what it looked like, God had the final word. All of this happened towards the end of December in the year 2009 and at the beginning of the following year we were moving back home to Texas.

It was time for the family to move again out of Oklahoma and this time it would be for good. My cousin and brother in the Lord finally received his degree from Oral Roberts University as well as my other brother Martin sometime before. God let us know in His own way that we had fulfilled our purpose in Tulsa and it was now time to go. We experienced a lot while living in Tulsa, Oklahoma that is a novel in itself. But I will say that it was definitely a learning experience. One of the highlights would be that my cousin finally received his degree and his grandmother my aunt left Texas (which I have never known her to do before) got to see her grandson walk with a degree in his hand. It was a beautiful moment. Sadly to say not long after she witnessed the historic moment of her one and only grandson graduate college, she passed away. She was the sister to my grandmother and one of eleven siblings to my big momma. And she played a big part of holding my mom's side of the family together in peace. My brother Martin also lost his grandmother while living in the Sooner state. So this place was bitter sweet, but the most important thing about living here was that we all got to know each other in ways that allowed us to grow physically, emotionally, and spiritually.

The beginning of two thousand and ten brought on many changes. The biggest one was moving back in with my mom in her one bed room apartment with my wife and three kids, what the hell? I was not feeling it at all and was truly crushed in spirit. I knew in my heart that the Lord had promised a financial blessing for us, but He didn't say how He was going to do it or when. So after a few weeks of living with my mom in her tiny apartment I prayed to the Lord this prayer:

Father I come before you asking you for forgiveness of our sins. Help us learn from our mistakes and guide us to make right choices and decisions. You are our God, the creator of heaven and earth and the beginning of all creation. There is nothing too hard for you and your ways are beyond our understanding. Your people will only prosper from your hand; salvation only comes from the Lord. You called me to be a leader of your people chose me to be a light amongst the darkness. Why must I struggle so much with wealth when the world is yours, when you called your people to overcome what is evil and to go possess the land? What is it that you want me to learn with this financial struggle? You passed down power to those who believe in your Word and the power of your Word is beyond comprehension. Lord you have broken every chain that held me back from knowing the fullness of you. You allowed me to acknowledge my faults, correct them and work them out for my good. You changed my thoughts, attitude, temper, anger, lusts, and behavior around to reflect yours. Now I asked you Lord to allow us to possess the land you gave to your people as a sign of your goodness and your faithfulness. Do not hide your eyes from those who have put their trust entirely in you Lord. Do not allow those who prosper in wicked ways and laugh at your servant's misfortune to do so any longer. Those who say there is no God He cannot do wonders; those wonders found in your Word done long ago. Help us Father! Bring us out from below the rock out of misery and distress, depression, and lack. For we are faint and are losing all hope, we are crying out for your hand Lord. We have said we are not poor not a child of God and yet we are poor. We said we do not have financial troubles; for everything the Lord has created is His and He lifts those who trust in Him from lowly places. And yet we have financial troubles, we are low without a place to call home. But I will put my trust in you Father. Show me what I need to do to carry out your will. Let us rejoice in the Lord and we will praise you in all the earth. Glory belongs to the Lord, majesty to our God. To you be honor forever O Lord. In Jesus name I pray. AMEN

We stayed with my mom a few more weeks after that. And in those weeks the courts wanted the child support that was due from me as a result of the paternity test. I needed to find a job, but it wasn't long before my cousin, my brother Ceasar came back from where he had moved in phoenix to deliver a message. Before I get into that I swore that after what happened with my family in the times I stayed with my granny both with and without my wife, I would never go back there. But that was exactly the message my cousin brought and one of my worst fears, having to face my dad again in the situation that we were in. So while my cousin was still in town getting his car ready to go back to Arizona I made the decision to go back with him to Sweetwater to stay with his mom in my aunt's house. This would turn out to be an interesting decision to make. His mom had talked about us coming to stay with her, but somehow it became a miscommunication on my part. After we got there what I thought she meant and what she actually meant where two different things. In short she never meant for us to stay with her for any amount of time or long term. It was pretty obvious the way she blamed her son for us being there. I told her it was clearly my fault and that if she wanted us to go we would. I believed in my heart God wanted us to be back in Sweetwater once again, He just didn't say how. Anyway a long story short, after my cousin left for Arizona all hell broke loose in that house. And what the devil meant for evil God turned it into good. The very next day after Ceasar left his mom she caused a big commotion, and I fell right into the trap. I had an uneasy feeling all morning, but I could not put my finger on it. Then it happened, one word lead to another and eventually true colors came out about how she really felt about us staying in her house. She was right she had every reason not to let us stay in her house, but it was how it was handled. I tried to keep my cool as best as I could from the way she came at me. Until I could not take any more of the belittling and she was in charge attitude. I told her in the beginning that we would leave if she wanted us to, but at the end of the day she pretended that it was ok. In the end she called the police on me to come get me and my family out of her house. This all stemmed from miscommunication and it did not have to go that far, but it was God's will. If it was not His will it would not have happened the way that it did. In a small town word travels fast because before we could even get our stuff out of the house good, people were already watching from up the street, and relatives was coming to see what was going on. It was quite chaotic and peaceful all at the same time. My uneasy feeling even though we were being whisked away to the police station with no other place to go, was gone. My dad's house would have been the one other place we could have gone. But due to the nature of me and my dad's background and that we got into it on the phone over money after we first got into Texas, he denied us access. But while we were sitting at the police station with nowhere to go the Lord spoke to my heart and told me to call him anyway. So I did and at first I didn't get an answer, but I left a message. A few hours past still no answer, so I tried again and then my step mom answered the phone. All communication went through her. My dad did not want to talk to me and he was not letting us go stay at his house. My step mom relayed that message quite well when she said, "do you think your dad is going to let you come stay in his house the way you talked to him on the phone." I had called my dad after we had been back in Texas at my mom's house for some help with a little money so we could get a few things we needed. Especially for some help with a suite to go look for a job, but he said no. The only other time I asked my dad for help dealing with money after I got saved was in Tulsa. After I entered a poem competition and they accepted me to go to Las Vegas. He told me no for that, but in that case I'm glad that he did because it might have been a scam. Nevertheless, all of the other times I asked my dad for some money if and when he gave it to me, was before I came to know the Lord. If you have any kind of relationship with God, you should know you cannot hold someone's past against them. People do and can change for the better, this was my case. But people who do not change for the better only remember the bad in the people who do. I am not here to bash my dad nor am I here to justify what I did in my past, I am only an offspring. And the apple does not fall to far from the tree. I will say this, I considered my ways and learned more in my relationship with the Lord about myself and my dad in ten years than I had my entire life. My dad was not all that bad at times. I do believe we had a loose connect of communication and understanding of each other. This was more than likely do to not spending a lot of time around each other. One year my grandparents bought me my first car. It was a yellow 76 Camaro and my dad helped me build it into a hot rod. He even gave me one of his engines to put in it. I was like a kid in a candy store and the envy of many after it was all said and done. So my dad had his good side like all people do. We just did not know how to relate to one another on different levels.

We had spent most of the day just sitting at the police station. Then they finally said that they could put us in a hotel room for a night maybe two, but that was the best they could do. My wife had even called her dad for some help, but heard the same thing I did with my dad. In fact the response she received back was that she and the kids could come, but I could not. I told my wife that she should go and that it was up to her if she wanted to or not. She decided to stay and at this point all we had was each other and our Lord and Savior Jesus Christ. Because no matter what we were going through the world was still turning and we were still breathing, which meant He was still in control and everything was going to be alright. The police took us to the motel and on the way they stopped by a church pantry in order to get a supply of food and diapers. Despite the circumstances this was a blessing from God, so after we got to the room we waited. The following day my Aunt Jimmie and Uncle Robert called us and wanted to know if it was alright of they stopped by to see us. I wanted to see family and also get help, but because of the drama with my own dad and even my cousin after she put us out of her house. I did not want to be going through anymore unnecessary drama. My aunt and uncle new we needed help and despite what they thought about our current situation. They were willing to reach out and try to help us and the kids. Let me cut to the chase here, God orchestrated this whole ordeal. If it were to go any other way it would have, but He wanted it to happen the way that it did. The steps of a righteous man are ordered by the Lord, if that man is willing to put the Lord's will above his own pride. There is no doubt that God will put you in very uncomfortable situations in order for Him to get the glory from that situation. God will also put you in situations to make you grow and test your faith. It is all about the Lord and I was being put in a situation for Him to demonstrate His power. This is what happened. My dad did not allow us to move in his house. But my aunt and uncle had a house they were willing to donate to us. My dad eventually came around to see us as well as my aunt and grandmother. They all pitched in to extend the stay of our motel room and supply us with more food and things we needed for the kids. At the same time they were trying to figure out a place for us to stay to get us out of that motel room. My aunt and uncles house was turning out to be more work to move in than expected, but if they were willing to let us have the house I was willing to put in the work for us to stay in it. At the end of the day my step mom and aunt worked out something with a longtime family friend who had a vacant house. She was willing to let us temporarily move in until we could get our feet on the ground. This was a blessing, she said it wasn't much, but it was a house and she was letting us live in it pretty much rent free until things got better. My dad immediately started helping me around to find a job and bring my truck back from my mom's house in Abilene so I could find and get to a job. I must have put in for a job all over Sweetwater without much success at first. But this is how God works; the very first job I received was through the pastor of my dad's church. And I didn't even have to go looking for it, because it came to me. It was funny. All of that searching for a job around town and then land one in a few minutes from a phone call, God is good. The job was a janitorial position at a wind turbine facility. I worked this job for a little over a month and then the Lord opened up a door for me at a local gypsum plant. This would be the ideal job for me and my family in my small home town of Sweetwater. It was not much to do in this sleepy little town and it was a great paying job, the perfect place to save some money. I also had to keep in mind what God was calling me to do as well. And He was also reminding me, maybe the very reason that while I worked this job I didn't have any peace doing so. If a person has any type of relationship with the Lord you know with everything within your entire being if you are in a place that lines up with the will of God. If not, then I tend to get a very uneasy feeling inside of me to the core, and a monkey wrench was about to be thrown into my machine. Although this job was a good paying job in return it was also taxing on the family. Production was sky rocketing and talking to some of the other employees, so was their attitude about working so many hours with maybe one day off. I on the other hand raised concern and asked about all of the work days and hours. The next thing I know I was being escorted out of the plant and asked to come back to talk to the HR department about my job. Long story short, because I raised concern they said that I was not working out and despite the short hands they had, they let me go. Now I have made mistakes before and this time might have been a mistake on my part indeed, or was it. I mean I had a good paying job and a family to look after, what was I thinking about opening my mouth up to spend more time with them. I watched and talked with some of the employees and their family life, if they had any, was struggling or in trouble. But then again was their family grounded in the Lord? However this was not about them this was about me and mine. And all I knew is that I wanted to spend more time with them that was my excuse. I mean how could I teach them to live the way Jesus wanted us to live if I was never around. Was I fired from my job because it was the will of God or was it all from me? Since I tend to control my own path at times instead of letting God be God and He "do what He do". It could have very well been my own fault. But even if it was my mistake God knew I was going to make it before I made it and already calculated my next move. Speaking of my next move I was already in an emotional state for even being back in my home town and did not want to come back. Due more to the fact that for me it was better to be around people who did not know who I was and they believed in me. Than to be around family and people who knew me from my past that didn't believe in me or what God was calling me to do. I mean they saw the transformation the Lord did in me, how He took me from near death and jail to reading the bible on a daily basis. And yet I was treated like a black sheep from following and having a relationship, not religion, with my Lord and Savior Jesus Christ. In their eyes I could have been viewed as a failure. I didn't have a house of my own and I had a family to take care of now without a job.

Before we even moved back to Texas my wife and I was making plans believing in God to move to San Antonio. But like everything else when dealing with a relationship with the Lord, He directs your path not you. Case in point after I lost my job this was the perfect opportunity to pack our things and head for the Alamo town. I heard God saying to my heart that it was time, but I also heard Him say why San Antonio just before we started to pack up and leave. Now I was stomped, because we had planned quite a while for this move. This was supposed to be our final destination. And yet the Lord said, "why San Antonio?" So I asked the Lord where He wanted us to go if it was not San Antonio, because I did not have a clue at this point. Very clearly and without hesitation the still small voice inside of me said "Dallas." So I prayed and I made sure that I was not about to make another hasty mistake, and all the Lord would say was Dallas. I accepted the fact that it looked like our journey was heading east and not south, but I needed conformation. We had to get some clothes dried at the laundry mat before packing them up so I went. On the way there I passed a big Greyhound bus and clear as day its destination was Dallas. Now because I die daily and yearn to get closer to the Lord as my priority, I have become very sensitive to Him speaking very loudly in subtle ways. This was clearly the conformation I was looking for and like the beginning of my relationship with the Lord; I stepped out on faith and headed for Dallas. On the way there we stopped by Mary's house to take her barbeque pit she let us use and to give her the keys back to her house she graciously let us occupy. On the way there we past my dad, but everything in me told me to keep going, because up to this point all I received was the third degree from losing a good job. Especially in a town where good jobs are hard to come by not to mention the economy and being in a small town, reputation was at stake as well. The Lord said, "Keep going." And so we did with the clothes we could pack in our bag the five of us headed for Dallas. We did not know what part of Dallas nor did we know where we were going to stay. All I know was that I was operating in faith, the Lord was my covering, and my family was following me as I was following Jesus. Everything had to work out. Was He not God creator of heaven and earth Author and Finisher of our faith?

Even though I had family living in Dallas the Lord was not leading me to seek any of them out for help. So I went to an area I was familiar with where my cousin Ceasar lived after his dad passed away, Grand Prairie. As soon as we settled in the hotel room the next day I went and got the paper to start looking for work. This was Dallas Texas surely there were enough jobs in the metroplex to get us started before the money ran out. Turning to the employment section I answered an ad in the paper, 'call today start tomorrow make up to twenty or thirty dollars an hour.' It was just what we needed to get on track, or so I thought. So I called the number and talked with a person who told me the location, contact person, and what time to be there. We were going to be on our way. We had a day or two before going up to north Dallas for this job interview. So we continued to look for other jobs and just kicked back and relaxed from all of the physical and mental drama. I was really starting to feel the effects of it all and if it had not been for my wife supporting me in a physical and mental state, I would have lost it. Spiritually I was getting stronger, but physically and mentally I was getting beat up like a rookie in the boxing ring.

The day before the interview we decided to pack up and head up to North Dallas to go and find the company, and then get a motel room close by. If I prepared today the chances of being late tomorrow would be slim. It didn't hurt to do your homework not to mention we needed this. After we found the company we went to check into a room close by. It was a far cry from our last room, but it was cheaper and it was a big difference. Since we did not have any cooking utensils we had to rely on a microwave and a mini fridge to get us by. Well this room did not have either and since we were trying to conserve money, not to mention it was getting low, we kept eating out to a minimum. However in this case we had to, it was the only way. We were also expecting another check from the gypsum job to come through to add to the reserve, my last check, and it would be just in time. But the day came for the job interview and I was ready to make some money for us in our new city. I got to the interview and checked in and it was really looking promising, until I found out that it was a mass hire and it was a commission only job. I was a little down at this point because I was not any good at trying to convince people to buy a thing. Either you wanted it or you didn't that was just how I looked at it. Anyway most sales jobs are ten percent truth and ninety percent lie especially those that where all commission. If the people did not buy what you had you did not eat.

So what would you do to put food on your plate if it came down to it? It was not something I was willing to do in the long haul. I never was a good liar even before I was saved I sucked at lying so this job was definitely a challenge. Despite the obstacle I stuck with it for as long as I could to try to get a check. I just kept praying Lord you're in control of all things and if it is your will for me to succeed in this, I will. Meanwhile we got an extended stay room with a kitchenette and a full size fridge to keep us tight while I worked this job until something else came along. Now I knew for a long time that God was calling me to be a minister, but it had only been four or five years that I accepted His will for me. So I decided for us to go to church and seek out the Word of the Lord and clearly find out what He had to say. Out of the many churches that we could go to in Dallas the Lord put on my heart The Potters House. Once again I was so zealous for the Lord and clearly motivated by my own agenda ready to do God's will. We ended up joining church that day. In my spirit I felt the Lord telling me not to, but I was not trying to make any more mistakes; like that was possible for me to do. Anyway I quickly found out that it was not where the Lord wanted us to be. Not because it was a bad church, it was merely the fact that I was getting ahead of God. And despite what He was calling me to be and what my circumstances looked like I needed to wait on Him.

The sales job was not working out. I went from door to door trying to convince people to get what we were offering. Everything in me was losing hope, especially when the money just about ran out. Something had to give. I continued to trust in the Lord. Then He began to speak to me and all He said was, "its time." I could not afford to go back to the sales job anymore and we only had enough money to stay one more night in a hotel. So we started looking for an alternative solution, then the Lord put on my heart to find a homeless shelter. We started looking in the phone books and so not to move in haste, we downsized hotel rooms for one more night while praying and sleeping on our next move. We had been in Dallas now for about a month or more and at this point I decided to call my granny to let her know that we were alright and not to worry about us. The next day we got up facing the inevitable with only about a hundred dollars left in our pockets and three little mouths to feed, we had to find a homeless shelter. We started off by putting in homeless shelters in the GPS on my cell phone which lead us to downtown Dallas. So we parked downtown in the West End district to find this shelter and we were getting frustrated. Where the GPS was telling us to go and where we were at was not a homeless shelter. So I called the lady and then called her back again and she finally gave me the right directions. Turns out they moved to another place so we went walking that direction. I put in the new address and it was not that far, but when you have three little kids all in the same stroller at the beginning of July in Texas, and you do not know where you are going, our walk seemed like an eternity. We searched and searched for this homeless shelter and everything began to weigh on my mind, I was becoming discouraged. While I was pushing my three little ones in the stroller with my wife tagging along right beside me I saw writing in the sidewalk. And it simply said remember Jesus loves you. It was that little piece of sidewalk that renewed my hope in finding the shelter. So I began asking people if they knew where this place was and with a little help we found it.

Walking up to it was mixed feelings, because it did not look like a place I wanted to take my wife and three kids under five years old. But we asked to speak to a counselor on how to get in and waited for a good hour or more outside before anyone came. While waiting a lot of the homeless people were talking to us and telling us how beautiful our kids were. And that we did not want to stay in this place because there were sex offenders who stayed. I did not want to either, but I felt like we had no choice because we did not have any other place to go. A van pulled up to hand out sandwiches and drinks which was indeed a blessing since our last meal was breakfast. Then the counselor finally came out to see us, took a look at us and told us the same thing the other people had told us. She said that we needed to try a place called Dallas Life Foundation down the road and pointed us in the direction. There was another homeless guy that seemed to just stand by us and was really making me nervous. It turns out that while she was giving us direction he was listening and offered to show us where it was. Even though I was tired and frustrated the Lord was still looking after us even in our worst situation. So we walked on heading towards the Dallas Life Foundation homeless shelter praying Lord let your will be done on the way. We finally walked the three or four blocks and arrived at the shelter just around the time they started new arrival check-ins and dinner. Since we finally found the shelter I took the opportunity to go and pick up our truck we parked at the West End. It turns out that it was much closer than the first shelter we were looking for in the beginning, God is good. So we entered in through their metal detectors and before starting the check-in process we ate in the kitchen. They told us that families had to sit in a certain section and single men and women had to sit in their own separate sections, so we did. But before we could sit down good to eat what they had served us. We were interrupted by even more disturbing news than what we already had been through. A lady came to our table and asked us if we were married and we said yes. She asked us if we had our marriage license with us and we just looked at each other and told her no. But we had told her that we had been together over five years, these are our three kids, God said she is my wife, and in His eyes if she was that is all that mattered. She told us that didn't matter without a marriage license I could not eat with my family. If we stayed I would have to go to one floor while my wife and kids went to another floor. I was not having that at all we came here together and we were going to stay together no matter what. So as hot as I was about the situation I got up and started to walk out and without even saying a word my wife followed. If there was any proof of how loyal a wife could be no matter the circumstance, she was showing it at that very moment. We had no other place to go, it was getting dark outside, and we barely ate any food before we left. And yet my wife followed me out of a shelter that would provide her with a roof over her head and food; that's loyalty.

So we got back in the truck and started heading west on I-30 and got off at a Cockrell Hill exit to get a few burgers to eat on at the McDonalds there. We did not have enough money to get another room and no other place to go as it started getting late. We had no choice but to sleep in our truck that night in the McDonalds parking lot. As I tried to get comfortable along with my wife and three small kids in this full size pick-up truck, it became real small real fast. We were all sweaty from walking all that day trying to find the shelter and reality set in with us that we were experiencing homelessness in a very real way. And yet with no roof over our head, Gabby, Manny, and Miah then three, one, and six months had finally went to sleep. All I could do was pray and continue to trust in the Lord God Jesus Christ who gave me hope and kept me from breaking down altogether. I could not help to think that this was my fault, that I put us in this situation. Then the Lord put on my heart that the king's heart is in His hands and that his steps are ordered by the Lord. I did say eleven years before that if God would heal my body and give me a wife I would go, do, and say anything He wanted me too. If I was in the wrong He would let me know it, but if He gave me peace in every situation even a chaotic one, then I knew it was God who orchestrated the whole thing. Even my mistakes would be turned into blessings if I stayed loyal to The Most High God no matter what it looked like. So I ministered to my wife that night and blessed her, because I knew God had us in His hands.

The next day we got up looking for other places to go, not finding anything, once again the Lord saying no more wasting time. He put on our hearts to go and get our marriage license with the very last of the money that we had left, which was less than a hundred dollars, so we did. We had found our way to a small park somewhere in Dallas. Now we were going to find our way downtown in order to take care of a little business. My wife and I both knew that we did not want to spend another night in our truck especially with the kids. And we both agreed that maybe this was God's way of saying that it was time. Time to make everything right, not only in the sight of God, but also in the sight of man that way we would be unapproachable. The next stop would be the county court house.

It was almost noon, and we started making our way through the process of getting our life papers. By the time we filed all of the necessary documents and got everything in order for the judge it was close to four or after. We knew that if we did not get this done today it was going to be another night sleeping in the truck. Failure was not an option and at this point it had to get done. Because after all of the filing fees we did not have any money left not even enough to sleep out in the truck and get food. So we started looking for a judge who would marry us and sign our marriage license. It was only after five years of being together, God telling me that she was my wife, and three kids later that we finally decided to make it official. But who am I to judge, even myself and our situation. It was happening the way God wanted it to happen if He wanted it to happen any other way, it would have. It was getting close for everyone to go home for the evening and we had gone to several floors and judges without any success. I was frustrated, tired, hungry, dirty, and only minutes away from giving up. That is when Jen kicked it into over drive and kept going, kept us all going. She was determined to find a judge who would sign our marriage license so we could get into the only homeless shelter that would keep us together in the same room. Time was running out and at the end of the last hour we found one thanks being to the Lord not a moment to spare. By the time we got out of the court house we had minutes to get back to the homeless shelter to check in before the cut off time. On the way out we thanked Jesus all the way and we knew it was His will. Throughout the hallway, there were signs that simple said it's about time. We just looked at each other and smiled while in a hurry to get to the homeless shelter to lay our heads. With one obstacle conquered it was time to face the next one, the transition into a homeless shelter, a shelter that would ultimately prove to be a growing place for the whole family.

This homeless shelter called Dallas Life would definitely become a challenge for us all. It would force us to think outside of the box, not only in our minds, but physically as well. The moment we checked in we knew that we were not in Kansas anymore. And it was like walking into a prison environment for the whole family. So we checked in and they gave us five free nights to decide if we wanted to join their ten month "New Life" program or work to stay for our room. The new life program was really geared towards people with drug addictions, but because we had no other option with the kids, we joined. Despite not having a drug addiction this was God's will. And even if we did not have a drug addiction, we had some type of addiction that the Lord wanted to address. This was our time to know ourselves and God on another level. This was our time to let our light shine in the darkness. This was our time. There was no doubt that Dallas Life was a homeless shelter, but what caught my eye was that it was also faith based. I found out early in my walk with God that just because people know that there is a God, does not mean that they have a relationship with Him. And in this place it was not any different. It was geared toward knowing the Lord, but not everyone who worked here did. It would be the perfect place for God to discipline His real kids and pass judgment on those who messed with them in one way or another.

One of the first challenges we faced right off the bat was that people who join the new life program had to work for thirty days in an environment like the kitchen. Not only did my wife and I work in this kitchen, but we also had to do it without being able to leave the property for the entire month. Part of their "detox" program for anyone who needed to get clean from drugs or alcohol, I had been a user of both and I knew people reacted differently to either one. I also knew that without a solid foundation like the Lord, the chances of someone being completely set free from drug and alcohol abuse was slim. For me, if it had not been for that initial relationship with Him. I more than likely would have died in my abuse of or dealing them ten years prior. The next challenge we faced and also part of the program was that we had to put our kids in a day care. This would not have been that bad if we had already decided to do so, which we had not. And if they had already been to one and they had not. So being forced to put your kids in a complete strangers care cold turkey was just as bad if not worse as trying to quit a hard drug without help. Let's just say I was not happy about the whole situation. I mean our kid's life was short lived, but the entire time they had only been around us. And at the end of the day it was not the peoples program that had me upset. God was the one who wanted to change our perspective on who we allowed around our kids. And it was He alone who would protect them. So as we went through the first few months of the program one by one the kids transitioned into the homeless day care system. I am so glad they did not go all at the same time. Because I don't know which one was harder us letting them go or them having to go. I believe in the end it was beneficial for all of us. The kids met new friends and we as parents, especially my wife, got a break from them for part of the day. The first one to go into the daycare was the smallest one, Miah, and it did not take her very long to adjust. She was only about seven or eight months old so she did not cause a whole lot of drama. On the other hand the second to the oldest, Immanuel, when it came down to his time to go he was not feeling it at all. Manny was just about to turn two at the time and he put on the biggest drama show of them all. He did not want to stay at the daycare at any cost. But we had to let him go. And just leave him up there every week for about a month or two until he finally adjusted. Our oldest, Gabrielle, now she was the one ready to go to daycare. After we went to check our other two in she wanted to stay too, play with all of the kids and the cool toys. Gabby was the one who was the most excited about going to daycare and we were relieved after Manny's stressful situation. However, when it finally came time for her to go, after her first day the excitement turned into fear. The ready to go three year old suddenly did not want to go anymore after being left at the daycare for a day. The next morning she caused a scene, but it did not take her as long to get over fear of being left at the daycare as it did her brother.

Part of the New Life Program at Dallas Life was to attend Chapel service on certain days throughout the week and also classes. Some of these classes would be substance abuse classes or faith classes. Either way God was trying to bless us through this place, through these classes, and being around new people. And being that I had a strong opinion about what I learned, who I learned it from, or even how they taught what I learned about God did not matter. All God wanted to do was bless us in this place and be a blessing. I started to let what they were teaching get in the way of us receiving what God was trying to give. Speaking up about how each person has a different perspective on the Lord (if they had one at all) and forcing someone to follow Him in your way of teaching is not the way to change a person's life. I mean how can anyone come to Christ if they cannot see Him in the person trying to get him/her to come to Him. And then we say, "This is the way you have got to go." But then they say if Jesus acts like that then no thank you. Simply put a person cannot be forced to do anything. You can put a choice in front of them but it is up to that person which direction they want to go. It is only two choices you can make, a good one and a bad one. Both of them I made based on the information that was giving or not giving to me at that particular time. This kind of teaching and strong opinion just about got me, and more than likely, my whole family booted out of Dallas Life. Who was I a nobody off the streets trying to tell one of the instructors of a facility how to do his job. I was not going to embarrass him in front of everybody else about the difference of his perspective and mine, and it was not my time. It was not yet my season. I had to bite my tongue and roll through all of the bad perspectives including my own. He was not the only one I faced confrontation with about the teachings of God's Word at Dallas Life. There were guys and girls that came through with way more education in the Word than I had, and at times, I could not relate to what they were talking about. The knowledge of the word was there, but where was the actual relationship? As if there teaching was automated, it was like speaking to a voice prompt asking you to press a number to get you to your destination. Cold and lifeless was what some of the teaching was like and I ran into a guy that was teaching some off the wall stuff. I mean big words and all it absolutely did not have anything to do with a relationship with the Lord. To me it just had to be a test and everything in me told me to say something. I had been doing good keeping my mouth shut trying to get through this whole nightmare, until that day. I could not believe what we were being taught and I looked around the room watching the people's faces being awed at what this guy was saying. The whole time he was using his big words I was thinking to myself no way. I had a real relationship with God and His Son Jesus Christ and my spirit was bearing witness against this man and his teaching. The Lord allowed me to speak and I told him that, "what he was teaching had nothing to do with people coming to the Lord. You are teaching these people what you have learned in your school and it has nothing to do with how we are to live our life for the Lord on a day to day basis. In other words you are teaching big words we have not heard before, but you lack showing how to have a relationship with God and then maintaining that relationship." The people in the class wanted me to shut up and let him finish, but of course they also just wanted him to finish. Most people that went through this program just wanted to work the system so they could get what they wanted and move on. I on the other hand really wanted to know God and show others how to know Him based on what He had already done for me. Despite the fact that we were living in a homeless shelter, we still believed in the Lord. That was the difference between knowing the Word and living the Word, showing the Word instead of telling the Word. All glory belongs to The Most High God none of it by how much we know or how elegant our words can be. God alone makes a man's mouth and the words that come out of it, but it should be up to God how we use it, not us. The only way I was able to do that was to just keep my mouth shut when I felt everything in me telling me to do so. It was not easy when you had a fire burning inside of you wanting to share with people what the Lord had taught you, especially without formal education. But education does not teach you to have a relationship with God, only faith does. And without faith it is hard or not even possible to get the Lords attention.

My family and I spent nine months in the Dallas Life homeless shelter. We met many people going through different things in life, we talked with them even spent time outside of the shelter with them. But there was one man that God used to show us favor at Dallas Life whom I will not soon forget. His name was Reverend "Ike" Johnson. Rev. took to us as soon as he saw us in the facility and wondered why we were even in the building. Clearly he could see we did not have a substance abuse problem. But I did have a problem with learning things the hard way. And sometimes your bad choices and decisions can lead you down the wrong path. It is even harder when you have a family who is following you down that same path. And that was one of the things the Lord was showing me. That it was a choice I made that got us in our homeless state in the first place. And yet that homeless state would be a teaching as well as a testament experience in our faith walk with God. No matter how bad I messed up God was able to turn the negative situation into a positive one. The only thing is I just might have got there faster if I had taken the time to do it right in the first place. Well there is no looking back unless you are reflecting on how God brought you through a thing. And should of would or could of is nonsense, only enjoy your journey of life on the way is relevant. Mistakes will always be made, but it's what you learn from those mistakes that matter.

By the time it came to the end of our lesson at Dallas Life homeless shelter. My wife and I had given our self and time into doing what God wanted us to do. We did what we could and left the rest up to the Lord Who brought us through. Part of the shelter program was to find a church home to go to before we could graduate the program. My wife and I met a wonderful woman by the name of Mrs. Craig who taught one of the classes that we went to in the program. Mrs. Craig was a blessing for us, God used her to open doors for us and she was also a member of Oak cliff Bible Fellowship Church where Dr. Tony Evans is pastor. We as a family decided to look into this church and after going a few times decided further to join, believing it was the will of the Lord. However, still knowing my calling I did not know how long the Lord would keep me in one place. At one point in time I just wanted to settle into a church and become part of a family. God on the other hand had a different plan for me and there was not a thing I could do about it, unless I decided to quit. How could I just stop doing what God had started in the first place? I mean I did not choose to be a leader. This is something the Lord chose, all I did was say yes to God and He in return said I was a prince. Ok, how do I respond to that? So I just kept pushing putting one foot in front of the other. Then the Lord revealed to me one day a king would return to lead his people in truth. He would not compromise, but speak boldly, and he would also fear God above everything. He would prepare the way for the return of the King of kings and the Lord of lords. This would be the man God had been searching for. And this man would be the one God would choose to lead His people. How does God determine a leader? What did he see in Moses? What was on his mind when he looked at David's heart or had mercy on Noah? No one can understand God unless God wants him to, and then I do not believe we fully can while still walking on this side of heaven.

About three months before we graduated the "New life" program at Dallas life I knew we had to start looking for a place to live. I did not have a lot of money saved up from my part time job at UPS, another requirement for completing the program. The other requirement was to find full time employment, but the Lord did not bless me in this area yet. Anyway God put on my heart to sell the only form of transportation we had at the time, the same truck my grandmother helped me get years earlier. So that's what I did. I sold my truck in order for us to have the money we needed to get into the place the Lord had shown us. As much as I liked the truck and really wanted to keep it to fix it up; it had served its purpose and God wanted me to let it go. I had peace about letting it go and I knew that if He blessed me once He would bless me again. God never does the same thing in the same way. So I knew the next time it more than likely would be a far greater blessing. What made this easier and harder at the same time was that we received news of another life blessing from God. We no longer had room for a full size truck. It was time for something bigger.

It's funny how the Lord works out every little detail in your life, including the ones that you don't see coming. My mom called me one day talking about us living together in a big house out of nowhere. I did not know what to think of it at first and then it hit me this was the will of the Lord. She saw it as being tired of where she was at, responsibility of being on her own, and not having someone to talk too. But God saw it as its time for you to draw closer to me and I am going to do it in a way you will never see coming. And that is exactly what happened. We needed to make a certain amount of money to get into the place God wanted us to get in, and my mom was the final piece of the puzzle to make it happen. At the end of the day my mom moved to Dallas and we got into the place the Lord intended. God is an AWESOME God indeed. Was it the end of the journey, by all means no, in fact it was just beginning.

My part time job at UPS though it was a job, was not enough to keep us where we were now living. Not long after we moved into our apartment the part time money I was making was quickly leaving. The government started taking child support out of my check off of the top. So I didn't even get what I was supposed to get that qualified us to stay in our apartment. The job my wife had applied and interviewed for fell through. And now we were in a frantic search to find jobs In order to keep the apartment we just moved into. I was already spending two hours going and four hours coming back from my job a day on public transportation. It got to a point where I could not even afford to go to work anymore. I even asked my mom if she had a few dollars so I could get my ticket. But then the Lord stepped in and said "I do not want you to go anymore." So I stepped out on faith again and did what the Lord asked me to do; voluntarily quit my part time job. I had no idea what we were going to do. We had rent and bills due and the only income we had at the time was from my mom's monthly check. It was hardly enough to keep us afloat and yet I didn't trust in the little we had. I trusted in the Great I am for everything. Whatever God was about to bring us too. He was about to bring us through it as well, no matter how bad it looked. Between my wife and me, we applied for jobs we were over qualified for from fast food to janitorial without a call back. I even made the decision to go learn how to drive a truck on a long hall to pay the bills. And yet God didn't even allow that, because they denied my application; I didn't even have a serious traffic violation. At this point I knew it was just the will of the Lord for us to go through what we were going through.

It had been two months since I had been out of work we were already behind in bills. And the first month of being out we already reached out to our church for help in paying the month of August rent and light. But God was not finished yet. We went through all of August and September before He gave me another Job. By this time Jen was due with our fourth child and he came very fast. The time came so fast with us both not having a job that we had no time to act negative about the whole situation. And on the fourth day of September we were blessed with our fourth child, a son. We named him Isaiah after the prophet, because we knew that God was our strength. And salvation comes from the Lord only.

After we received notices for late rent we finally let the apartment office know of our situation even as we faced being evicted. They asked if we could come up with five hundred of the rent, so I asked my mom since she had the only income at the time. Well at the end of the day she said she didn't so we were back at square one. It seemed since I didn't have a job my mom had giving up as well. And decided to do with her money what she wanted instead of doing more to keep a roof over our head. But just when all hope seemed to be lost I got a call from the unemployment office for a job interview with a record management company. I knew this had to be a door opening from God and I was going to walk right on through. They had a two interview process and I made it to the second out of twelve people. I knew this had to be God, because this was a full time job and it came just in time. In the meantime the two months I was out of work was devoted to writing this book about my life. And speaking what was on my heart in relation to what God was and is doing in my life. We are still in wait for what God is going to do concerning our next move. We still live in the apartment complex we moved into after the homeless shelter. And we still face being evicted if we do not move out soon. My co-worker made a call to a person he knew that worked at an apartment complex in Oak cliff just down the street from the job. Our current apartment complex suggested we move verses being evicted. So after being approved for the other apartments, we are just waiting for an open unit. Grant it that it is not as nice as the ones we stay in now and the rent is more, but all bills are paid and we get a fresh start. No matter what it looks like though God said that it was time to prosper and that our season has come. What comes after that only God knows, but God is a BIG

God not some pretend figments of our imagination that can't make things happen. He makes all things happen whether good or bad all we have to do is believe. But in all of this and despite what was going on. I still did not have any peace about moving out of the current place we lived in. So I called out to God and asked the Lord, "is it your will for us to move Lord?" and God spoke a word to my heart and simply said, "No". At this point I knew deep down inside that God was going to give us what we needed to stay in our current apartment. And indeed that is exactly what happened despite my issues, short comings, and plain old rebellion from the living God. He is GOOD, He is AWESOME, and He is FAITHFUL to His Word even when you can't see all that He has created, like money. We may not always be able to see it or even possess it in our hands or bank account, but it does not mean it is not there. It just means God is testing us to see which one we will chose over Him, money or the Lord?

At the end of the day after you have done all you can and all of the money is gone. Family remains the most important thing in the world. Money is temporary and will only last as long as you can hold it, but family can go with you to your final destination. Hopefully that final place will be with the Lord providing you kept the faith, belief, and relationship alive with Him throughout the days you walked the earth. As for me and my family, we may not have the "American dream" of having a house with a fence or even a car and a stable bank account. We may not have the bling and all of the fancy material things you see on TV society portrays you should have. But what we do have is a relationship with the Lord God Jesus

Christ who created it all. And we have each other, which is the most important thing, through good times and bad time's poverty and prosperity those things do not stop us from functioning as a family. Money does not define us, only the Lord defines who we are as individuals and as a family. And it is God who will keep us together as a family through thick and thin, not money.

We will defy gravity and move to a place the Lord intended our family to go; towards Him. And we will do it with or without money. It is God that keeps us together not money or material things. The devil is destroying families by any means necessary, why? Because he knows family is why God created everything for Himself. Without the Lord families do not function properly the way He intended. Since the Lord is the Prince of peace and the devil is the lord of chaos, the one we choose to follow will be the lord of our house. We marry then we divorce, we cheat, and we beat each other in front of the kids. We humiliate one another and talk down to each other just because we think that we can. All of these things we let Satan do to us because we refuse to let God be a part of our life. But without God we have no life, Jesus is our life. Without Him we are like a sheep waiting to be slaughtered and at the same time living in utter chaos.

As for me and my family, the chaos stops with Jesus Christ and being real with ourselves and the Lord. Even when we run into trials and tribulations God has saved us right when we thought the suffering had beat us. I still owe child support and between my wife and I we owe, still are in debt. But we are not going to let money break up the family God has put together. We are still going to believe in God that what He has created He has for us and if He has it for us no one else can take it away. We just have to continue to train in order to receive the Lords blessing's, especially those that can potentially harm us instead of do us good like money. Because it is said with more money comes more problems and that is definitely true if you are not mature enough to receive the type of financial blessing God is capable of giving.

At the end of the day we are still blessed, because we have a relationship with God who gives the blessing. I do not believe in luck or karma, because those things do not dictate whether I win or lose. I believe my outcome is based on the choice or decision I make at any given moment in time. But more important understanding what God's will is for me in any situation is going to determine that outcome, not luck or karma. At the end of the day we do not have luck or karma. We just have God, the Lord.

Thank You Jesus, AMEN!!!

CONCLUSION

Today is October 16, 2011 and I as child of God still have debt and struggle financially after walking all these years with the Lord. God told me years ago that He was going to pour out a financial blessing so big I would not be able to contain it. What He did not say was what I would have to go through to receive that financial blessing.

Today the financial struggle ends. Not because I have come upon a large sum of money or have won the lottery. But it is because I'm still believing in God and His Word and commanding my financial struggle to end. It is time to take a stand and prosper as God has commanded His people to do those who choose to have a real relationship with Him.

I shall now prosper; my family shall prosper in all things, because we believe in the Creator, the Great I am. Even though we cannot see it we believe it, because God has said it, that's faith. This has been my entire journey all along, FAITH, dare to walk in it.

If you are struggling with issues in your life that may even be threatening your very existence as I have (don't get it twisted I am still working out my issues with the lord). And you are still breathing, then it is not too late, God is calling you to have a relationship with Him. All you have to do is accept Him in your heart by believing in His Son Jesus Christ. Believe that He lived to show us how to live a life before God and then died on a cross for our sins. Believe that God raised Him from the dead and gave Him the seat at His right hand side to give us eternal life. By faith you will receive the gift of the Holy Spirit and be saved. If you believe in your heart that Jesus Christ is the Lord of lords and the King of kings the One and only true God.

It's a simple process and all you have to say out loud or in your heart silent is: Father God forgive me of my sins I repent Lord wash me in your blood. I believe by faith you sent your Son to die on the cross for me and then raised Him from the dead so that I may have eternal life. I believe in my heart that it is through your Son Jesus Christ that I can come to you and have a relationship with you. I'm letting go of my fears and the pain people have caused me in the past that has kept me from having a relationship with you. Come into my heart Holy Spirit and fill me with your unconditional love. Teach me how to live a life according to your will. In Jesus Name I pray. Amen

This is only the beginning if you prayed this prayer of salvation. God is going to create a new you and you are going to go through some things as I did. Keep in mind God is a God of change and your results may vary from mine, yet the outcome will be the same. I went through what I went through because it is I you will go through what you go through because it is you. It is not always gloomy with God the sun doesn't shine to make us stronger. The more adversity you go through the stronger you will be and the higher your calling will be in God. Just remember all great leaders had one thing in common. No matter how hard the trial, they never gave up or quit. Stand for something or fall for anything.

May God bless you, your family, and anyone you come in contact with on a daily basis?

Forgiveness

God has forgiven me for my sins, my wrong doings, because I asked Him too. So because He forgives me for all of the wrong I did against Him. I am forgiving everyone who has done me wrong at any point in my life. I forgive my dad, mom, my brothers and sister, all of my kids, my grandmother, and grandpa for their role in my upbringing or the lack thereof. I would also like to forgive my granddad and granny, my first wife and all of the women I have been with or around. All of the friends I had and still have, I forgive you. I pray that you will find it in your heart to forgive me for all of the wrong that I have committed against any of you.

If God can take a little old country boy from a small town and turn him from being a sex-addict, drug dealer/user, with a bad attitude, temper, and full of pride around. To being a positive influence and inspiration to people who have lost hope in this world, for His greater good. Then He can do anything with anyone, there is NOTHING impossible for Him. You can be forgiven for your mistakes.

Do not worry if things do not work out the way you planned or envisioned. Because God's plan and His vision will always succeed, if we allow it too, all we have to do is exercise the patience the Lord has given us. In order for us to wait on and receive the blessing He has already given in our hearts.

WISDOM MY FATHER TAUGHT ME
Change My Perspective
Change My Life

How I look at things is going to determine my reality. If I have a negative perspective on life going through a bad or negative situation (also known as the fire) is just going to breed more negativity. I call it a bad attitude on life and that is exactly what I will get under whelming results. Take electricity for example it works by taking positive electrons and putting them with negative electrons they collide and give off energy. It is the same way with our perspectives. If I go through the fire with a bad perspective and a bad attitude all I am going to get is just a bad situation. But if I go through the fire with a positive perspective knowing that this is for my growth which is for my good then I come out a stronger vessel. And like the positive and negative electrons that create energy, so does my positive attitude in a negative situation. I now can begin understanding the situation that in the end is bringing energy and growth. Electricity will not flow with two positives or two negatives. Neither will I grow if I continue to look at my negative situation with a negative perspective or attitude. So how do I change my perspective?

The more I let God change me and how I see things, the more things will change around me. In fact it is not that the things will change around me, but that I have learned to let go of all that unnecessary stuff. I have now been able to change enough on the inside to change everything around me on the outside. Now I will no longer look at myself in the same way again and not only myself, but others as well. This is how I change my perspective; this is how I change my life. There is nothing more I want to do than to learn how to love God and to give Him more of me each day. Each day I give myself more to the Lord the more God reveals Himself to me in ways I never thought that He would. Above all else there is nothing but God. How much I give to Him is how much comes back to me and then some. Do not expect to get anything if I am still holding on to what I need to give. My whole heart is what He desires; my whole heart is what I need to give.

Believing, Doing, And Speaking God's Word

I heard a word today dealing with God's Word. And though God's Word cannot be simply put, simply it was said to decree God's Word. That is what they said in other words speak what has been written. But what they didn't say was before you speak, believe what has been written. Before you believe do something to change your present circumstance and before you do something, believe. Which brings us back to the beginning believing that God can do what God said He would do for those who what? Believe. And not just believe, but believe in His Son our Lord and Savior Jesus Christ.

Believing in God goes beyond comprehension. You cannot possibly believe in the unseen if you are thinking about believing in the Lord, you just have to do it. Putting aside all of the pain you go through from your growth is absolutely essential if you want to put God's Word to work. There is nothing more stifling of His Word than putting your pain above Him. It is fear that allows us to do just that, put God second. Now we have to kill fear itself so it doesn't interfere with what God is trying to do in our lives or put Him second. The only way to kill fear is to admit you are afraid in the first place and let God deal with it. And yes, for you to know you are afraid of something. God will throw you in the fire just so you will know He is not playing. Passing God's tests can only be done with God. Religion will not pass them for you. Only a real relationship with Him through His Son will.

Let me use myself as an example. Right now my wife is pregnant we have three other children and I have no job. Uh Oh the fire just got hot what do you do? I admit my first reaction was to worry and ten years ago it would have been to panic. But God has saved me from other fires. So I do believe if He did it then He will definitely do it again. My secret is that I truly believe and trust in the Great I Am. This confidence did not come over night and it is a gift I constantly perfect on a daily basis. How do you do that you may ask? Well when you have gone through so much with a person you will get to a point where you will just throw your hands up and say "Do whatever you want". This is the key, the more you go through the more you are able to let go. (Hint: the more you are going through the greater your service to God.)

Most people give up because they lose faith, cannot take the pain anymore, and just stop believing. Fear sets in and takes over quick. When you get to a certain level in God you cannot take your eye off of Him even for a second, because if you do it only takes that second for fear to take over. So after you reach a certain level in God you have to without a doubt remove yourself from what you use to do yesterday and the people you use to be around. Even if they say they claim to have a relationship with God sometimes you have to remove yourself from them until God brings you through your test. They do not have the same relationship with Him as you do and more important they may not believe in Him as you do. And also God may not be calling them to a level as He is calling you. So they will not relate to what you are going through and in return may even pull you away from reaching your break-through.

BELIEVE IN YOURSELF

Believe in yourself, no matter what circumstance we find ourselves in, no matter where we come from or where we are going, no matter what education level we have, no matter how tough life gets, believe in you. But in such a chaotic world full of deception and lies and in what that lie creates, the brokenness of all people.

How do you believe in yourself in such a deceptive world? How do you believe in yourself after all the lies we have been told or have told other people? How do we believe in ourselves after we have been hurt by so many people? The enemy tells us that we will not succeed at anything or that if we do not do what he wants (by controlling our actions) we will fail. He sticks his head up and sneaks into our lives so deceitfully that by the time we have noticed, it's too late. We have just become victim to a wrong choice in life that will affect us from one generation to the next.

How do we overcome every fear known to mankind? Because it is fear that drives us to lie. It is fear that causes us to talk down on one another. It is fear that puffs us up and makes us think that we are the most corrupt homie in the land and that no one can stop us. It is fear that tells us that we cannot when God tells us that we can. But there is no fear in God, for God did not give us a spirit of fear.

There is no fear in love. But perfect love drives out fear, because fear has to do with punishment. The one who fears is not made perfect in love. (1 John 4:18)

The fear of the lord leads to life: Then one rests content, untouched by trouble. (Proverbs 19:23)

So how do we overcome fear? We put everything we have into trusting our Lord and Savior Jesus Christ. If we believe that God exists and that he gave his only Son for our sins then we should believe all the way and not part or halfhearted that God can deliver us from anything. God wants it all not some part or half, but all of our hearts. He wants us to trust him in a way that in no matter the circumstance we know with all of our being that he will save us out of every trouble even though chaos is right at our front door. That is how you overcome fear get thrown in the fire stay there for a while and simmer and see don't God come and pull you out before you burn. Well how do you know that Calvin, because he has done it many of times for me and my family as you have just read. Yes I am a witness to the power and saving grace of Christ and not only I, but my wife and though they do not understand right now my kids also are a witness, He is no joke.

God is the only source who will allow you to believe in yourself in such a way that only He can. First of all He will show you how to be content in your own skin. You will not need to look to others for approval or admiration He is all the approval you need. Second of all He will show you how to let go of years of pain in order to see Him clearly, you will need to clean the murky water. This will be entirely up to you, because this you will have to want to do. And the only way you are going to want to do it is if you get completely tired of your own mess. Third we have to let God be God. How can we being mortal made by God tell God how we should run our life? Does He who has made all things not have it (all things) under control?

How can we say we trust God if we do not allow ourselves to give ourselves completely over to him. In other words how much of our lives do God influence? One arm, two legs, three fingers, or is it the whole body from the inside out? I believe one of the first important keys in believing in you is to believe in the God who created you.

Change My Perspective See the Bigger Picture.

With all of the chaos and disaster happening around I believe the best thing we can do as believers is change our perspective of the situation. Instead of focusing on why is this happening why not focus on the bigger picture.

God you are allowing this to happen for a reason Lord. Give me the strength, understanding, and patience to help me understand and see the bigger picture that I need to get out of this situation that you have allowed to happen.

And instead of trying to get out of a heated situation which God has done on purpose for His purpose let's stay in the fire. Why Calvin? Because in the fire is where character is forged. In the fire is where our hearts is fine-tuned and strengthened and sculpted for Gods will and purpose. So do not be so quick to jump out of the fire the Lord has put you in, if He put you in it He will take you out of it when you are done.

When you first pull out a puzzle it gets tossed out of the box and on to the table. Once on the table you start shuffling the puzzle pieces around and turning them over so that you can start finding the right pieces to put it together. After sometime and you have shuffled all the pieces, turned them over so that you can start putting them together then you start seeing the whole puzzle or the bigger picture. It is the same thing when God allows a chaotic moment to happen in our lives. Just like the puzzle we get shook up and tossed on the table, we get turned over and moved around. But in the end when God is finished fitting all of our pieces together we find out what He intended for us to look like—the bigger picture.

Sometimes God has a very unusual way of getting us to a certain place where He wants us to be. And the method that He chooses to use we might not always agree with it and it may even seem cruel, but in the end it always works out the way God wanted it to work out. And though all of the pieces of the puzzle are all scattered around with some turned over and on the floor just like our hearts at times if we allow the Lord to finish the puzzle, in time what a beautiful picture we all will see. This is all for the Glory of God and to be a witness to His Majestic Power Jesus Christ.

Suffering For a Greater Good

I have sought you Lord with my whole heart and each day brings a new level of faith. As I examine myself looking closer at those things that are inside of me that are not like you. Take all of those things away Lord, show me how to have a deeper relationship with you God. I don't want to get caught up in going after things in this world, even though you have created it and we share in your creation. It is the Creator I am determined to seek after and not any form of pride in creation in the world. How magnificent you are Father and even though we cannot see you we see you everywhere and in everything. And so we suffer just as your firstborn Son suffered many years ago on the cross for our sins to redeem our souls from eternal hell. And just like Jesus who came from heaven to walk the earth as a mortal man to be an example of how we should be before you Father. How He suffered amongst the hands of men, I too suffer amongst the hands of men to be a witness of your Son Jesus Christ and to be an example like Him in sharing in His suffering not only for believers, But none believers as well in hope that they may see your goodness even in the mist of chaos and confusion and utter misfortune. Even in times of trouble you are still God and you allow us to go through hard times to strengthen our hearts in preparation to fight against the enemy. You said in your Word our struggle is not against flesh and blood, but against the rulers, against the authorities, against the powers of this dark world and against the spiritual forces of evil in the heavenly realms. (Ephesians 6:12)

If this world is dark then this world must be your enemy and if this world is your enemy then this world are my enemy and or the evil things in it. And all I desire is you and those whom believe in you and who are called out of darkness.

In Jesus Name I pray,

AMEN

It's Time to Destroy the Lie and Live Again

Leaders of a higher calling, it's time to step up and stand up for what is right. Defend those who cannot defend themselves, help those who cannot help themselves, and speak for those who are too weak to speak for themselves.

It's time to up hold their cause. No longer can we be silent and accept mediocrity, we can no longer be Luke warm. It's time to raise the temperature on our thermostats and not be afraid to say what needs to be said for our physical, mental, and spiritual growth. The world today and the people in it are based on a lie. And it was not so in the beginning from the One who created it. It's time to stand up for truth and lay down the lie that has corrupted so many lives and families. Our homes are being broken (the body we live in) the collapse of the real estate market is a representation of the breakdown of our physical and spiritual body. In return entire families have split apart due to financial struggles. Struggles that never stood a chance because it was based on conditions, and with conditions there is always a hidden agenda, and with a hidden agenda there is always a lie. Love is unconditional. It stands above everything, better yet it just stands. Everything else falls around it, and is contaminated by the waste.

It is time to stop wasting time and start cleaning up the mess that has caught everybody off guard. We will believe a lie before we will even listen to or accept the truth. This is unacceptable, because when something goes wrong in our lives we walk around with our bottom lips poked out like a little kid who did not get his way. The next thing you know we are taking it out on someone else because our feelings are hurt. This too is unacceptable, as believers it's time to stand up for our own mistakes and stop blaming others for how miserable we are. Or maybe you are just not a believer. We need to stop treating people bad just because we have been treated that way. You cowards stop running from yourselves. We make people believe we are one way in our actions, but in our hearts we are corrupt as a thief in the night. Let's start putting an end to all this foolishness. No man can blame another man for his rise or fall, you are the blame. You rise because of your attitude and you fall because of your actions. It's time to stop pointing the finger and start creating the dream. We need to start building again, but first we need to tear down old bad habits and traditions. And this time when we build, build on a foundation of truth. So that when the earthquake comes our structure will stand after all hell breaks loose. Destroy the lie and live again . . . .

THERE IS NOTHING TO BE AFRAID OF, IF YOU HAVE NOTHING TO HIDE.

Eleven years ago I entered into a relationship with the Most High God through His Son Jesus Christ. Ever since then it has been an uphill battle to get to a point where I would be afraid of nothing, but God. And be completely free of having nothing in my life to hide from myself or anybody else except well of course, God.

There is good in everyone, but sometimes the evil that is present inside us as well wins. The enemy does not want you to succeed, in fact the more we try to do well or the closer we try to get to God the stronger the opponent becomes. He knows what God has in store for you more than you do. Take for instance before I was saved I had a problem with sex, in short I was addicted to sex. Well guess what? After I was saved I still had an addiction to you guessed it, sex. The problem did not go away just because I was saved. It was only covered by the grace of God until I was mature enough to find out and go after the root of the problem. Turn it over to God and then let Him deal with it like only He could. But before I did that,

I thought that I could handle it on my own by not fighting what I thought was the root of the problem, which was having vivid porn shows in my head from past relationships and pornographic films I had seen in the past to deal with the problem. Well um the Lord showed me real quick that was not the way He was going to handle one of my biggest fears. See that was the way I wanted to handle it or the way I thought He wanted me to handle it. Boy was I ever wrong, because that was not what God had in mind. God came to me with a word so strong concerning the matter that I was upset about it for a long, long time.

But see God showed me that I can't fix a problem on my own, because I was the problem. Only the Lord can fix a problematic situation in my life I just had to be willing to let Him. The only downside to that is unless I believe in him in the first place there is no way I would let Him do anything in my life anyway. Keeping on the subject fear will cause you to lose track of everything. And what I mean by everything is God. So when I was afraid I lied and tried to hide from myself and everybody else every troubling issue I had. The problem with living in fear is that no matter where you go it will go with you. And fear will explode on anything it can get its hands on co-workers, family, and even your own kids. I remember taking a swing at my son when he was a baby because he would not stop crying and I was trying to work on some music. This was of course before I was saved and it was the grace of God even then that I did not hit him. But that just goes to show you how fear can operate in a person's life. The devil uses fear to get you to operate out of character and fear uses you to carry out the action. Fear can be an all-out noticeable feeling, but most often fear has a very subtle approach to it and in most cases you don't even know you're scared of something until it is too late. Take for instance a seven-teen year old gets in to it with another kid on the street and they begin to fight. The fight escalates even higher and one kid pulls out a gun on the other and begins to pull the trigger. We do not need to know what happens next all we need to know is this is fear in action. The fact that these guys got in to it in the first place was because they both feared one another. For one reason or another one or both had something to prove and that was the beginning of their fear which led to the fight which led to the shooting. Without God we will never learn to control our fear or even recognize fear and what it can do to us before it's too late.

Here is the good news. Every time that we do something out of character the devil laughs and rejoices out of fear. But God laughs and rejoices at the devils expense because He knows that every believer in His Son is strengthened by mistakes and adversity. The greater the struggle, the greater the responsibility you have.

WHY AM I NOT WHERE I OUGHT TO BE IN GOD?

God himself reveals the secrets of a man's heart. Who can hide what is inside his heart from the Lord? The person himself does not even know what is all in his own heart. So how can he know unless he asks the Lord to reveal the inner most secrets of his heart to that man! And how can he ask unless he desires to have a relationship with the Son of God? No man can come to have a RELATIONSHIP with the Lord Jesus Christ unless the Father draws him near. (John 6:44)

The foundation of everyman is his heart, if the heart is not right there is no way a man can be. Everything ever created started with a foundation. If you look at a building going up, it starts from the ground up. The earth is leveled, the concrete is poured and then you have to wait for some time to pass so the concrete foundation can get hard in order for the building to stand. But let's go back to the leveling the ground. Now I'm no architect, but I believe a building needs to have balance in order for it to stand. Otherwise a ground that is not level will cause the structure to lean to one side or the other eventually causing it to fall down over time. So in short without balance a building cannot stand. And so it is with Gods most precious creation, the heart of man. Balance is the key to any healthy relationship. For God says, 'make level paths for your feet and take only ways that are firm.' 'Do not swerve to the right or left.' (Proverbs 4:26, 27) (Isaiah 26:7) (Proverbs 11:1) The Lord abhors dishonest scales, but accurate weights are his delight.

Psalm 111:10

10) The fear of the lord is the beginning of wisdom; all who follow his precepts have good understanding. To him belongs eternal praise.

The reason why we serve or swerve to the right or left, why we cannot be still, is we do not have a fear of the Lord. We get caught up in selfish ways; selfish motives that we fail to focus on the Creator and when we fail to focus on the Creator we instantly kill everything around us including ourselves. When we kill, after a murder is committed-we run. The first thing a person wants to do is run away from the problem. When we do this we are constantly on the go always looking over the shoulder. Because we are always thinking that someone is out to get us for what we did or are doing. **Are we guilty or not guilty?** It is the same way when we run from ourselves. I run away from me when I do not know how to love myself. If I will **not** allow or do not know how to love myself, how can I love anyone? My issues begin with me. All of my problems and negative ways of thinking all begin with me. When I do not know how to love myself I will hurt anyone who tries to hurt me or worse hurt the one who tries or wants to love me.

This is the message you heard from the beginning; we should love one another.

1 John 3:11, 12-24

Hurting people hurt people, but in Christ there is freedom. Jesus died on the cross so that we can be free. Free from sin, free from rules and regulations, and free from ourselves. But I'm so caught up in my own issues and problems that I cannot see the blessings of the Lord right under my nose, even if it is the simple fact that I woke up still breathing and able to thank and praise the Lord for another day. Wow the little things we take for granted . . .

Matthew 7:1-5	judging others
Matthew 22:34-40	the Greatest Commandment
1 Chronicles 28:9, 10	serve God whole hearted
Psalm 51:10	create in me a pure heart
Psalm 139:23, 24	search me, O' God
Proverbs 5:21-23	a man's ways are in full view
Jeremiah 29:13	seek me with your whole heart
Jeremiah 17:10	I the Lord search the heart
Matthew 5:8	blessed are the pure in heart
Matthew 6:19-21	for where your treasure is
Matthew 12:33-37	from the heart the mouth speaks
Romans 10:9, 10	with your heart you believe

1 Kings 8:56-61   praise be to the Lord
1 Kings 8:22-53

Genesis 9, 12   the beginning

September 4, 2010 3:18 A.M.

WE ARE AT WAR

We are at war. But the enemy is looking right at us as we stand in the mirror. My worst enemy is not Al-Qaeda, Satan, or even my next door neighbor. My worst enemy is myself. Defeat him and we win. Let frequent prayer run your life, not every now and then chaotic moments. This is where the war will be won.

DEDICATION

This book is dedicated to my family, friends, and people all over the world who are struggling in life changing situations. I hope that it inspires you to keep going when everything in you is telling you to stop. Never stop believing in yourself or our Lord and Savior Jesus Christ the Almighty God of us all. May He bless you and you bless Him in all that you do. AMEN

When you are going through your day to day living ask yourself, how strong would I be without all my struggles in life?